Miroslaw Matyja

Utopia or Chance?

Direct Democracy in Switzerland, Poland, and Other Countries

„*The Swiss have shown spectacularly that there is a difference between what is said at the local pub, and the opinion of the people.*"

Heiko Maas, German foreign minister

FOR MY FAMILY

Contents

Part II
Direct Democracy in Poland

ANNEXES

Foreword

Multicultural, poor in natural resources, and mountainous, Switzerland has existed, essentially, in an unchanged form since the second half of the 19thC. In Switzerland, it is not one's slogans, origins, wealth, or skin colour that matter but, rather sound arguments and the protection of citizens. **After 1848, when the Swiss constitution was adopted, and the current political system was established, Switzerland transformed from a backwards and poor nation into a society that still enjoys an unparalleled wealth and political stability.** Due to bold systemic and institutional solutions, based on the instruments of direct democracy, as well as an advantageous economic situation and unique historical circumstances, Switzerland and its numerous ethnic, linguistic, and religious minorities, is able to deal efficiently with both internal and external conflicts.

The political doctrines of various countries emphasise that the idea of their direct democracy is mainly associated with the political system of ancient Athens and other Greek city-states. Today, however, it would probably be more precise to use the term "half-direct democracy", since it rarely happens that the two conditions that define democracy are rarely fulfilled. These conditions are: the unity of place and time, and the collective participation of the sovereign subject[1] in all stages of political decision-making (from the initial proposal of a draft to the final adoption of a bill). If we, however, consider the fact that the sovereign's[2] voice is the ultimate power in political decision-making, then the vast majority of the instruments that enable Swiss citizens to actively participate in this can be thought of as direct democracy.

Direct democracy has wielded an enormous influence on the history of Switzerland and its citizens. Nothing unites people more than the awareness of the fundamental value of their democratic independent rights and the protection of the jointly acquired wealth. This raises the following question: why has Switzerland – a wealthy country, located in the centre of Europe, with a long multi-cultural tradition– chosen such an unprecedented way of development?

---

[1]   Being a sovereign subject means having the ability to exercise power over a given territory, a group of people, or oneself in an autonomous, independent manner. Sovereignty of the state includes autonomy in both internal and external matters [author's note].

[2]   A sovereign is a political entity that exercises supreme, independent power [author's note].

While some people consider it a utopia, others see it as a real chance for a better future for Poland and hold to the idea as fast as they can. The idea we are talking about is direct democracy, a grassroots form of exercising power and a political system in which it is the citizens (the sovereign) that have the deciding voice regarding Poland's crucial issues.

It is generally believed that the Polish nation is not equal to this form of governance; that Poles are foolish and incapable of making binding decisions. According to this belief, they have no clue about politics, and all they do is consume goods secured for them by the ruling class, i.e., politicians whose most important quality is that they are a part of the system, regardless whether they lean left or right. The people in power are considered different than citizens – they have proper qualifications, experience, they bear responsibility for the country, and, above all, it is them who were elected in order to govern.

The idea of the average citizen deciding on the matters of the state is at odds with Polish reality. That is why direct democracy is considered here a utopia… But is that exactly the case? And where did the idea of grassroots governance, which a growing number of citizens considers as a chance for a better future, come from?

Well, politics is similar to sports: impossible is nothing. We remember perfectly that even in the '70s virtually no one in Poland believed that we would free ourselves from the chains of communism. Central planning and everyday dullness were meant to last forever. In the end, it turned out that the change of the political system – and the form of governance – was in fact possible and became a reality.

Sadly, however, the very concept of political authority is grossly misunderstood in Poland. It is generally believed that the ones in authority are unique individuals, the chosen ones, or celebrities elected to decide about our fortune or misfortune. Yet, the concept does not simply refer to individuals or cliques in power, but to a process of domination of one group over other. That is why Polish society could, and should, be its own authority since it is the sovereign and the owner of the Polish state.

Why is it then that in Poland 40 million people are ruled by a small, exclusive group?

The aim of this book is to propose a model of grassroots governance in Poland and to show that it is not a utopia, but (maybe) a historical chance for our country. It is important to mention here that **we are not arguing for a revolution, but rather for an evolution of the Polish political system**. It is an attempt to find a better and more efficient form of functioning of the Polish state that would make it closer to citizens.

The current Polish semi-democracy is criticised every day, and rightly so. Up to now, however, there has not been proposed any model that would include Polish society – as the sovereign – in the decision-making process and provide an alternative to the elitist, top-down mode of governance.

The goal of this work is to present a complementary model of the political system for Poland that introduces forms of grassroots democracy. The project is based mainly on the experience of the Swiss direct democracy, which means that the proposed solutions have already been tested and certainly are not utopian.

While reading the book, please do remember one thing: sharing the political power with citizens is not a charity on the part of the ruling class – it is a democratic right of the sovereign, i.e., the citizens.

Part I

Swiss Direct Democracy

Introduction

The Swiss success is a result of many political, economic, social, and psychological factors that, essentially, have aligned perfectly throughout the country's past.

First, Switzerland is a nation founded upon a political will, otherwise it would not have been possible to establish such a state comprised of different ethnic, linguistic, and religious minorities. From the very beginning of the Swiss statehood, the will of its founders and the principle of compromise has been its determining factor. **For the communes and the cantons were not only different but also at odds with each other. It was the political will, the attitude of compromise, and, consequently, the acceptance of one's political opponents' opinions that became the foundation of this system of direct democracy.** If it had not been for these national traits, the Swiss would have never succeeded politically and economically. These traits evolved throughout centuries of poverty, constant threats from neighbouring powers, and a multicultural coexistence marked by a long tradition of independent self-determination. The Swiss government (the Federal Council) is formed collectively and in a way that acknowledges the whole diverse spectrum of the Swiss. As a result, it is very difficult to quickly change any law since every bill may be put to the vote in a nationwide referendum. Thus, it is essentially impossible to suddenly change the political direction of Switzerland.

Second, the French occupation at the turn of the 18th and 19[th]C. had a positive effect on the development of the Swiss statehood. There are many examples from European and world history which suggest that being conquered, invaded, or occupied may foster the evolution of state's institutions and society's unification. A similar process happened with Switzerland when Napoleon took the full control of the country. As a consequence, a model of a state was established, which combined the Swiss tradition of grass-roots democracy with – due to Napoleon's influence – the principles of a law-governed state.[3]

Third, another factor that has positively influenced the development of the Swiss state is its neutrality. During the Congress of Vienna, in 1815,

---

[3]   A law-governed state is a state in which democratically made laws have the supreme position in the political system. It binds those who exercise power and demarcates their authority while granting citizens a number of rights and liberties. In a law-governed state, government agencies and institutions may operate only within the limits of law, whereas citizens may do anything that is not forbidden by law [author's note].

Switzerland gained the status of a permanently neutral power.[4] In its constitution of 1848, the country sanctioned its neutrality and defined the principle of the cantons' autonomy. It was a turning point in the history of Switzerland since it used to be fragmented by religious wars and inter-cantonal conflicts. Instead of joining international conflicts, the country focused on the protection of its borders and the preservation of internal order. The First World War was a real challenge for Switzerland. Although the country was neutral, the Swiss people expressed various sympathies, depending on their region. The Swiss who lived in French and Italian regions supported the Allied Powers, whereas the majority of the German regions supported the Central Powers. It was obvious that violating the conditions of neutrality and joining the conflict would cause a bloody civil war and the potential disintegration of the country. That is why the government constantly invoked the Swiss ideals and appealed for a national unity. Switzerland emerged victorious from that trial. The First World War, which devasted nearly the whole of Europe, had little impact on the country.

---

[4] A permanently neutral power is a state that remains neutral towards the participants in all future wars. It is not sufficient to declare neutrality in order to gain the status. Such a neutrality must be recognised by other members of the international community. Permanent neutrality is established through an international treaty or a decision of a given state acknowledged by the international community [author's note].

During the Second World War, Switzerland also remained neutral – mainly due to its advantageous geopolitical situation, well-equipped militia-type army, and its reliable banking industry that respected the principle of banking secrecy.

Fourth, an essential factor in the evolution of the democratic system of Switzerland is the wealth of the country. It is well-known that political stability is key to the economic development of a country, but economic growth and wealth also guarantee political stability. The maintenance of the system of direct democracy is highly expensive. This raises the following question: where did the wealth of this small, Alpine, and land-locked country that lacks natural resources come from?

The economic structure of Switzerland is based mainly on the chemical and precision tool indus-tries, tourism, export-oriented farming, banking and financial services. In the early Middle Ages, Alpine highlanders gave up farming and focused on breed-ing dairy animals, as well as the production of milk and cheese. That is one reason why Switzerland has become famous for its cheese and chocolate.

After the religious conflicts in Europe, French Huguenots came to Geneva, which was dominated by the ideas of John Calvin at that time. Since they specialised in watchmaking, their arrival marked the beginning of the Swiss watchmaking industry. Almost instantly, the Swiss started to export watches to wealthier European countries.

In the 19ᵗʰC. the Swiss Alps were discovered by wealthy Brits. They were the first ones to conquer the summits of the country and so began the age of tourism in Switzerland.

Towards the end of the 19ᵗʰC., in the industrial age, the textile industry was developed, which paved the way for chemical, mechanical, and pharmaceutical industries. The Swiss industry lacked any patent protection which, in partnership with low import duties, resulted in the higher competitiveness of Swiss products. In 1934, banking secrecy was introduced as a natural step in the development of the financial sector. These conditions, extremely favourable for economic growth, fostered the political stability of the country and attracted numerous immigrants, among whom were many entrepreneurs.

The real economic boom in Switzerland, however, started after the Second World War, when Europe, destroyed in the conflict, began raising itself from the ruins. Since the Swiss economy and industry were unaffected by the war, the country began a large-scale export industry to its devastated neighbours: Germany, France, and Italy. The Cold War also proved to be advantageous since many Western politicians and businessmen, as well as the "red aristocracy" of Eastern Europe and dictators from around the world used to deposit their money in the Swiss banks.

Fifth, the Swiss are diligent and take responsibility for their lives and communities.

They are stereotypically called a "police nation" because they meticulously guard their common good. Due to the fact that they take decisions concerning every area of their lives, they treat public property as their own. This attitude is reflected in politics, which is practiced most actively on the communal level. The Swiss learn about their joint responsibility for the common good from childhood and, as a result, become highly politically aware adults. The decisions made through referenda are not hasty but, rather, well thought out and based on the sense of common responsibility for oneself, the state, and the future generations.

The centuries of poverty shaped the diligent attitude of the Helvetic nation. The Swiss value work and cultivate the idea of it. Polls show that work is not only the source of wealth but also satisfaction. Moreover, the Swiss tend to value functionality over luxury. They are rarely impressed by material goods, and even if so, they do not show it. The responsibility for the common good is much more important than wealth, and work is a value in itself, not just a source of income.

Sixth, it is often forgotten how important the role of education is in the socio-political development of a country. In Switzerland, education is, not accidentally, considered to be a national treasure. The schooling system follows the idea of pragmatism and is based on two types of schools: general and vocational. Choosing one of them does not exclude the possibility of continuing one's education in the other in the future. For example, if a student graduates from a secondary vocational school, he may also complete a one-year skills improvement course and study an entirely different field. That is why the Swiss say that one can accomplish one's goals regardless of the initially chosen educational path. Furthermore, students do not learn business skills in higher-level schools but through practice. It is interesting that vocational and trade schools are more popular than the ones providing general education.

Seventh, the mentality of the Swiss plays a crucial role in developing and maintaining the system of direct democracy. Seemingly uninteresting, their mentality is characterised by calmness, composure, apparent slowness, acceptance of authority, punctuality and meticulousness.

It may seem strange to a foreigner that the Swiss direct democracy has proven to be one of the most stable political systems in the world. It would seem that giving the reins of the state to the people is a recipe for a financial disaster. However, the numerous examples of the Swiss referenda prove otherwise. Swiss citizens often have to take decisions on very bold and untypical matters such as: the extension of paid leave to six weeks, the introduction of unconditional basic income, or the dissolution of the Swiss army. The Swiss have proved that they are capable of governing their country wisely and far-sightedly without giving in to unrealistic slogans and visions.

To sum up, due to the following factors: centuries-old civil socialisation, political will of the nation, discipline and diligence, responsibility for oneself and the state, tendency to compromise, advantageous geopolitical situation, mentality, and education, the Swiss have worked out a functional political system that has no counterpart in today's world.

1. The Institutional and Historical Determinants of the Swiss Political System

1.1. The Beginnings of the Swiss Statehood

The history of Switzerland is undoubtedly the key to understanding the country's political system and the mechanisms of its institutions. The historical development of the Swiss political system is characterized by unique solutions despite the fact that – when compared to other countries – its history is rather short and "poor".

In ancient times, the area of the modern Swiss state was populated by Rhaetian and Celtic tribes. The name *Helvetia* comes from the Helvetii, the representatives of a Celtic tribe that settled in the Aare valley. However, the beginnings of modern Switzerland date back to the 1st of August, 1291, when three cantons – Uri, Schwyz, and Unterwalden – formed a confederation[5] and made an alliance in order to jointly

---

[5] A Confederation is a loose union of states based on an agreement made usually in order to pursue a common foreign policy. The states remain sovereign and, as a rule, there is no centralised power [author's note].

defend their lands against the Habsburgs. In this way, a so-called eternal union was made that would later become the foundation of the Swiss state.

This pact, known as *Eidgenosenschaft* – i.e., "a union made under an oath" – was confirmed by a special declaration, the so-called *Federal Letter*, which was also the first political act of the Swiss Confederacy. The citizens of the cantons, i.e., the signatories of the pact, expressed their belief regarding the alliance's permanence and declared mutual aid in defending their liberty and sovereignty. They also pledged not to recognize any settlements imposed on them by an external power and to settle any disputes by peaceful arbitration. At first, the document was classified. Its content was not revealed before the battle of Morgarten in 1315.[6] Later, it was lost and eventually found in an archive in Stans in 1760. The document was translated and published in German.

Throughout the subsequent centuries Switzerland's statehood developed, the Swiss political system underwent many changes, and the additional cantons and communes that joined the confederation retained their sovereignty.

A turning point in the history of Switzerland occurred in the late 18[th]C. when the French army,

---

[6]   The Battle of Morgarten – the battle (15 November 1315) in which the citizens of the cantons of Uri, Schwyz, and Unterwalden defended their rights to independence from the Habsburgs. It took place near Morgarten in the canton of Zug [author's note].

led by Napoleon Bonaparte, occupied its territory and destroyed the existing political and social order.

The direct cause for the French army's invasion were the inter-cantonal riots. In July 1798, undoubtedly influenced by the French Revolution, the citizens of the canton of Waadt – threatened by the authorities of the canton of Berne – sought the help of the Napoleonic army. After the fighting, Berne and the whole Switzerland was conquered by the French. On the 12th of April, 1798, in the city of Aarau, the constitution of the so-called Helvetic Republic was officially proclaimed. Based on the French model, it was established as a centralized, unitary state.[7] Drawn up in Paris, the constitution was an attempt at combining the progressive and enlightened ideas born by the French Revolution with the concept of a state, governed top-down, which – up to then – was a notion completely foreign to federal Switzerland. The changes introduced by the constitution of the Helvetic Republic were essential to the cantons' status and limited their competencies. The union of sovereign countries was replaced with a unitary state without any borders between the cantons, which, following the French example, were renamed as "departments".

---

[7] A unitary state is characterized by internal political and administrative unity. All of its administrative units are organised identically and subordinated to its central authorities [author's note].

1.2. The Political Situation Before 1848

In the summer of 1802, the French army withdrew from the Helvetic Republic by the order of Napoleon Bonaparte. The reasons were the Swiss' growing protests and the cold calculation of Napoleon himself, who expected the French to soon come back to the Republic as the saviours of a divided country.

After the French left, the Swiss could independently make attempts at reforming their state. However, even adopting the so-called Second Constitution of the Helvetic Republic did not put an end to the internal unrest and riots. The whole of Switzerland was ridden with rebellions and conflicts. The advocates of the cantons' sovereignty and the federal structure of the state rose to prominence. Due to this, on the 19th of February, 1803, Napoleon imposed upon Switzerland a new constitution – the so-called Act of Mediation – which revived the principle of federalism. The Act came fully into effect on the 10th of March, 1803, bringing an end to the Helvetic Republic and, as a result, recreating the former administrative structure of the state.

Therefore, the political system imposed by France did not survive long. Centralising a confederation of free states proved to be impossible. On the other hand, the Act of Mediation turned out more durable with its effects still visible even in 1848, when the new constitution was being prepared.[8]

The Act limited the competencies of the federal authorities to the following domains: foreign policy, military, ratifying tariffs, and mediation in inter-cantonal conflicts. At the beginning of the 19th C., these competencies belonged to the assembly of the cantons' representatives, and in the period between its sessions they belonged to the *Landmann* (the president), who also represented Switzerland abroad. At that time, however, the confederation's foreign policy was still strictly dependent on France.

It should be pointed out that the time during which the Act of Mediation had been in effect, the confederation experienced a political stabilisation. Due to being strongly dependent on France, however, Switzerland was highly sensitive to political events in other countries. The fall of Napoleon in 1814 also marked the end of the political system based on the Act of Mediation. The first half of the 19th C., until 1848, was a very difficult era for Switzerland. Great changes that occurred in the areas of politics, society, economy, and technology transformed the country's and its people's life.

---

[8] Especially in terms of separating the church and the state, standardising weights and measures, as well as establishing a common currency, legislation, and army [author's note].

The decision regarding the further status of the confederation was made at the Congress of Vienna, during which, on the 20th of March, 1815, the then Swiss state was granted neutrality and inviolability of its territory. The European powers agreed that a neutral Switzerland would be a perfect buffer zone between France and Austria, thus, contributing to the political stability in Europe. In the meantime, Switzerland regained its confederation's territories and, on the 7th of August, 1815, the 22 federated states signed an agreement – an inter-cantonal pact – that made Switzerland a federation,[9] as opposed to its previous status as confederation.[10]

Around 1830, political thinking changed to be more favourable to the idea of returning to a centralised state. There were also attempts at discrediting the inter-cantonal pact and the assembly of the cantons' representatives.

In the years 1830–31, democratic revolutions occurred in twelve cantons that lead to a replacement of the former authorities with modern democratic institutions. However, citizens still lacked a direct influence

---

[9] Federation, as opposed to confederation, is a state that comprises autonomous parts under a common (federal) government. The parts that constitute a federation have an internal autonomy and can make their own laws in certain domains. The common factors are, however, the currency, foreign policy, and defence [author's note].

[10] The union has used its traditional name – the Swiss Confederacy – as a reference to the alliance made between the three cantons on the Rütli mountain in 1291 (Ger. Schweizerische Eidgenossenschaft, Fr. Confédération Suisse, It. Confederazione Svizzera) [author's note].

on legislation and decision-making. Between 1831 and 1835, there began attempts at modernising the federal pact of 1815. In the early 1830's, many projects aiming at revising the pact were made but did not yield any positive results. Both the opposition during the 1830–31 constitutional debates and the social movements of 1839–41 demanded the right to veto political decisions. Today, this right can be considered as the precursor of modern referenda. The first veto was introduced in the canton of St. Gallen in 1831. As a democratic instrument, veto was not practical since it did not pose a threat to the liberal parliamentary democracy. The democratic opposition was still too weak to be able to efficiently utilise the right to veto. Finally, in 1848, the assembly of the cantons' representatives declared its own dissolution, which began the modernisation of the federal state and changed the 1815 pact into a constitution. The changes, later named as the Bern Project, were accepted by fourteen cantons and one half-canton. A city in which a given session of the parliament was taking place was temporarily considered the capital of the country.

1.3. The Constitution of the Swiss Confederation in 1848

In 1847, a civil war broke out between the Roman Catholic and the Protestant cantons. Catholics tried to prevent the strengthening of the central power, which was the goal of the then ruling representatives of the Radical Party. The hostilities lasted for a month resulting in about 100 deaths. It was the last significant armed conflict in Swiss territory. Since then, the country has never experienced the horror of war. As a result, in 1848, the federal constitution was drawn up, and its announcement marked a turning point in the shaping of the Swiss political system. The constitution introduced a system of state governance based on the instruments of direct democracy, while leaving the cantons and the communes the right to self-govern on local issues. In the new constitution, the state declared itself as religiously neutral and adopted the principle of territoriality according to which multilingual Switzerland legally acknowledged every language used within its borders. All linguistic communities acquired the right to be – proportionally to their size – represented in the state's political institutions. Thus, the first proposal founded upon the instruments of direct democracy became a fact.

The new constitution comprised of a preamble and three chapters that contained 114 articles, as well as interim provisions. The confederation of cantons was officially replaced with a federation whose members – the cantons – had to voluntarily give up a certain part of their sovereign rights in order to submit to the new power. The new federation retained the traditional name of Confederacy and obliged itself to maintain the unity of the Swiss nation while ensuring internal order and peace. In this way – after gaining competence in foreign policy making, declaring war and peace, organising the military, introducing tariffs, establishing postal and monetary systems – the federation claimed the right to intervene in the case of internal conflicts between cantons or a potential civil war.

Apart from guaranteeing itself international independence and internal peace, the federation set itself two main goals: the protection of the cantons' rights and liberties, and the pursuit of citizens' general prosperity. Among the cantons' competencies, the schooling system, judiciary, legislation and police remained. The union guaranteed all of its citizens freedom of religion, speech, and association, as well as the right to assembly. The essential fact is that, from the very beginning, the federation ambitiously intended to create a Swiss nation. In order to do that, the freedom to settle was introduced, which meant that every citizen of the new Swiss state had the right to choose a place to live on the federation's territory without the risk of losing any of their basic rights.

However, the most significant innovation introduced by the Constitution of 1848 was undoubtedly the establishment of the legislative and the executive arms of the central authority: the parliament, the government, and the federal tribunal. The parliament – the Federal Assembly – elected in general elections, was made up of two houses: the National Council, which represented the nation, and the Council of States (two deputies from each canton). An important novelty was the executive power, the Federal Council, that consisted of seven members representing different cantons, political parties, as well as linguistic and religious groups. The first Federal Council was elected on the 16th of December, 1848 and adopted a system of collective decision-making (the act of the16th of May, 1849). The first assembly of the two houses of the Federal Parliament took place in Bern, which was chosen to house the authorities of the newly established state, on the 6th of November, 1848. Since then, Bern has been considered as the seat of the federal authorities, though not as the country's capital in the proper meaning of the term. The term "capital" refers to domination, whereas the Swiss do not tolerate any elements of domination in either political or social life.

Apart from establishing the new state order, the federal constitution of 1848 included the possibility of amending it. The amendments could not only be made through the obligatory constitutional referendum,[11] but also through popular initiative, i.e., by the will of ordinary citizens. This set up the framework for the contemporary liberal government and its policy of modernisation. The constitution of 1848 should be considered as a declaration of will: at

---

[11] The Swiss constitution uses the term "mandatory" for the obligatory referendum and "optional" for the non-obligatory one [author's note].

that time, democracy and the Swiss nation, as well as the nation state and the federal system, were still being defined as the young state's goal – they were not yet a reality.

1.3.1. The Modifications of the Constitution of 1874 and 1891

The process of centralising and limiting the cantonal power in favour of the federal authority in Switzerland was not problematic. The cantonal constitutions could not include any regulations that would contradict the new federal order and had to provide the possibility to be amended at the majority of citizen's will. Those constitutions, as well as the Federal Constitution, were repeatedly amended between 1848 and 1874. The most important amendment was introduced in 1874, although – despite many changes – it was still a continuation of the political system established in 1848. The changes introduced in the new constitution focused mainly on transferring some of the commercial competencies from the cantonal level to the federal one and on allowing the unification of civil law, especially its commercial branch.

The 1874 revision of the Constitution was not thorough and it retained basic federal institutions, such as a bicameral parliament, the Federal Council, as well as regulations concerning citizens' rights and liberties. The modified constitution increased the competencies of the central power, specifically in military issues.

The Federal Government took upon itself the responsibility for the total of military affairs and commercial law. The federation gained a significant influence over religious matters. Also, the competencies of the Federal Supreme Court were expanded regarding the conflicts between the cantons and the central government.

The most important amendment to the 1874 constitution was the introduction of the optional referendum, which affected the development of Switzerland's constitutional system and the form of its political system as a whole. The amended constitution granted the central government essential competencies, but its decisions had to be implemented in stages since the authorities had to take into consideration the attitudes and the mood of the citizens taking part in a referendum. The amendments that extended the competencies of the Federal Council included the introduction of a common currency and changes resulting from the population growth and the industrial revolution.

Another modification was made in 1981. It extended the scope of the popular initiative, which, from that time, was not only to be used to adopt a new constitution, but also to introduce individual constitutional amendments.

1.3.2. The 1999 Constitution

The current Federal Constitution of the Swiss Confederation was enacted in 1999. When it comes to the position of the parliament, there were no radical changes; "…in this regard Switzerland remained faithful to its political tradition and retained the foundations of the system established by the constitution of 1848."[12] There was no intention of changing the political principles that had been proven for 150 years.

On the18th of December, 1998, the Federal Assembly proposed a draft of the new Federal Constitution. It was accepted by the nation and the cantons in the mandatory referendum on 18 April 1999, and it came into effect on the1st of January, 2000. In this way, after 125 years, the constitution of 1874 was replaced. It should be emphasised that the basic values of the Swiss democracy, such as federalism, direct democracy, welfare state[13] and liberal rule of law were retained and only adjusted to adhere to modern times. The fundamental principles of the 1999 constitution are: human dignity as the

---

[12] P. Sarnecki, *Zgromadzenie Federalne. Parlament Konfederacji Szwajcarskiej*, Warszawa 2003, p. 7.

[13] The welfare state principle is a political commitment according to which the state is supposed to provide its citizens with the basic means of subsistence. It also includes the task of evening up the inequalities between the rich and the poor through the principle of social equality. Providing a safety net for the old age and those at risk – e.g., in the case of disease, disability, or unemployment – are the foundations of the welfare state [author's note].

state's highest value, welfare state, free competition and subsidiarity.[14]

The constitution consists of a preamble and six clearly formulated titles:
- Title I: General Provisions
- Title II: Fundamental Rights, Citizenship and Social Goals
- Title III: Confederation, Cantons and Communes
- Title IV: The People and the Cantons
- Title V: Federal Authorities
- Title VI: Revision of the Federal Constitution and Transitional Provisions

The new constitution retained the "three-level" political system made up of the communes, the cantons, and the federation. Although the fundamental territorial and political units are the cantons, a lot of

---

[14] The principle of subsidiarity means that any authority, and especially the political authority, should play only a supportive (auxiliary) and stimulating role in regard to the efforts undertaken by autonomous and independent individuals who established a given authority. Wherever it is possible and necessary, the state should not deprive the people of their power (whether parental, official, or political on any level), which they can exercise on their own will and by their own means, and through which they can fulfil themselves for the general, as well as their own, benefit. Any social intervention should be primarily motivated with the intention to help the members of society, not to replace or thwart their own initiative. Encyklopedia PWN, https://encyklopedia.pwn.pl/haslo/subsydiarnosc;486984.html, [accessed 10 August 2018].

weight is attached to the political and administrative role of the communes.[15]

The fundamental value of the Swiss constitution lies in the fact that it does not question the legal identity of the cantons. As Bohdan Górski rightly states, "The constitution does not turn against patriotism or attachment to the regional culture and identity. On the contrary, it integrates patriotism into the federal system, where it is a great force in service of a given canton and the Confederation."[16]

As I have already mentioned, Switzerland is a very diverse country in every respect. This diversity is the source of the specific role of the constitution, which – unlike in other countries – is not only a normative act, but also the actual foundation of the integrational process and identity of the Helvetic state. It cannot be forgotten that the Swiss nationality is based on the will of its citizens. That is also why the

---

[15] The communal tasks include: appointment of the authorities, management of assets through agreements, public finance, imposition and collection of taxes, granting citizenship, primary and secondary public education, maintenance and establishment of educational facilities, appointment of educational authorities and teachers, public healthcare and social welfare, provision of commonly accessible non-specialist healthcare, provision of essential means of subsistence to the needy, maintenance of public peace and order, local planning, formulation of area development plans and issuing location decisions, organisation of public works, establishment, development, and maintenance of industrial services, as well as technical, cultural and recreational infrastructure [author's note].

[16] B. Górski, *Jak przeżyć kapitalizm*, Retro-Art., Warszawa 2013, p. 78–79.

principles expressed in the Constitution are of particular significance. Among other factors, they are the bedrock of Swiss patriotism, which may seem odd to other nations.

1.4. Summary of the First Chapter

Through the course of history, the Swiss political system has evolved, and its democratic nature has matured and improved. This process is still going on. Today, the Swiss system can be described as "parliamentary-cantonal." In 1848, Switzerland adopted the Federal Constitution and a system based on referenda, while local issues, such as taxes, judiciary, schooling, police, and welfare were left to the cantons. In 1874, amendments were introduced, which included the optional referendum. In 1891, the Constitution was amended once again, thus establishing a unique system, rooted strongly in direct democracy. The current Constitution of Switzerland was adopted through a referendum by the majority of voters in 1999.

The most important innovation of the 1848 Constitution – later amended in 1874, 1891, and 1999 – was the establishment of a political system based on some elements of direct democracy. It granted citizens a number of rights and liberties, including the freedom of speech, religion, and the free choice of the place of residence. The new political order was institutionalised according to the aspirations of the liberal-democratic cantons. The possibility to amend the Constitution – through a constitutional referendum, as well as the popular initiative – was introduced at the outset. This Constitution should be perceived as a declaration of will of its creators. Time has shown that the new democratic system, based on instruments of direct state governance with strong federal tendencies, was not just an imaginary goal – it has become a practical reality.

2. Principles and Functioning of Swiss Federalism

2.1. Federalism Through Integration

A federal state differs from a unitary one – i.e., one that is governed from the top-down – in that the former tends to transfer governmental tasks onto lower administrative and territorial authorities. The federal state's powers come directly from the people. In Switzerland, it is the people who decide about the form and the function of the state, which is founded on the communes and the cantons. These subnational units are federalised and deprived of only those competencies that they voluntarily and exclusively transferred to the federation. Nevertheless, the majority of the governmental power is transferred from the federal level to the lower tiers in line with the principle of subsidiarity. The territorial authorities that make up the federal state are granted such an extensive autonomy in the fields of constitutionality, legislation, executive and law-making that they can be virtually considered as separate states, although they lack any competencies concerning home affairs and defence.

Switzerland is the first federation in the world that came into being as a result of tightening the relations between many sovereign canton-states. Swiss federalism is therefore an example of a federalism through integration, while the name "Confederation" has merely a symbolic meaning.

Switzerland as a model of "federalism through integration" means that, in the moment of establishing the Swiss state, the cantons had to give up certain part of their competencies in favour of the new political entity. When discussing Swiss federalism, one should always take into account the specificity of this country. Despite its limited area, Switzerland is characterised by deep multiculturalism, with four linguistic regions and two dominating religions. The small size of the Swiss territory, as well as its cultural, historical, and religious diversity, have shaped the peculiar character of the country's federalism. Firstly, the Swiss rejected the idea of creating a monocultural state with only one official language and religion. Secondly, they managed to build a type of democracy that enables it to divide power not only between Catholics and Protestants, but also between the German-speaking majority and the French, Italian, and Rhaeto-Romance minorities. Therefore, it is a country characterised, by great will, by the building of an independent nation based on mutual respect for its minorities and citizens.

As it is known, nationalism is concerned with an ethnic tradition and the desire of part of a given country to become independent from its whole. In Switzerland, however, it was completely the opposite: citizens of the cantons, who represented different languages, ethnic and religious groups, developed a belief about the necessity of establishing a political entity that would not be based on the common tradition and culture, which, today, may make their country seem to be an artificial creation. In order to properly understand Swiss federalism, one cannot forget that the state comprises of twenty-six cantons,[17] which, to a large extent, are autonomous and proudly regard themselves as "republics" or "states." It is the cantons that are the foundation of the federation, and not the linguistic communities as it is commonly thought. All but four cantons are linguistically homogenous, which means that there is still a risk of a conflict if their citizens decide to form a separate faction of cantons. However, the conflicts between the cantons are very rare. One of the reasons is the fact that the boundary between the French-speaking part of Switzerland and the German-speaking one runs through three cantons that recognise two official languages. Another factor important for Swiss federalism is that the boundaries between the region dominated by one religion do not coincide with the boundaries of the linguistic regions or with the cantons' borders. Switzerland has

---

[17] The following three cantons are divided into half-cantons: Basel, Appenzell, and Unterwalden [author's note].

German-speaking cantons dominated by Catholics and French-speaking ones dominated by Protestants.

An additional important element is that Switzerland has no official capital. The federal authority has its seat in Bern but the Federal Court is located in Lausanne. Bern is ranked only as the 4th largest city in the country. Zurich, Basel, and Geneva exceed Bern not only in size of the population, but also in scale of industry and banking. The factors that foster the cooperation between the cantons are: the concentration of banks' headquarters in all major cities, the fact that all of the four linguistic regions have their own tourist resorts, and that the major factories are located in, at least, two linguistic regions. Since there are many links (linguistic, religious, economic, and cultural) between the cantons, the Swiss policy is characterised by forming many changeable coalitions that not only cooperate, but also compete. None of the coalitions create a long-lasting majority, and none of them dominate in any area. As Christoph Büchi rightly states, the battles for the *"Röstigraben"*[18] should

---

[18] The term *Rösigraben* was coined during the First World War when the citizens of the French part supported the Entente, whereas the citizens of the German part supported the Three Caesars' Alliance, with the German Empire as the leading one. Strangely enough, society's sympathies coincided exactly with the boundary between the linguistic parts of Switzerland, as if the boundary between the German-speaking part and the French-speaking one was also a mental barrier between two separate nations. Today, the term is used in in the context of analysing the results of referenda [author's note].

not be taken literally since the unity of Switzerland is guaranteed regardless of the outcome.[19]

Switzerland's entrepreneurship and economic policy flourish also due to its openness to diversity. Although Switzerland is commonly associated with specific products, like watches and clocks, chocolate, cheese and banks, the country's success results from the way in which various inventions and innovations, as well as the cantons, are linked with each other. It is this typically Swiss diversity ("a multitude in unity"), stemming partially from federalism, that marks the country's innovative character – from tourism, medical technology, production of chemicals and pharmaceuticals, to banking or the watch and clock industry.

An important aspect of federalism is the bicameralism of the federal parliament, which significantly differs from that of a unitary state's parliament. The Swiss parliament – just like any other parliament of a federal state – comprises of two chambers. The first one, the National Council, represents the nation. Its election and the distribution of seats depends on the size of the cantons' population. When it comes to the election of the second chamber, the Council of States, every canton is given two seats regardless of its population size (half-cantons are given one seat each). Even though the legislative procedure

---

[19] Ch. Büchi, *Röstigraben. Das Verhältnis zwischen deutscher und welscher Schweiz. Geschichte un Perspektiven*, NZZ Libro, Zurich 2000, p. 15.

can be initiated in any of the chambers, the enactment of a given law requires their mutual approval, which emphasises the significance of the cantons in federal decision-making.

It should be added that the Swiss engage in the so-called "federal dialogue." It is a forum used for regular political meetings (usually twice a year) between delegations of the Federal Council and the Conference of Cantonal Governments,[20] which represents the cantons. The goal of the federal dialogue is the harmonisation of the federal and the cantonal policy during the time of initiating and carrying out new projects. **The governing principle in this context is: dialogue is the source of a compromise.** One example is the construction of the Alpine Tunnels, partially financed by the federation, which required many difficult negotiations between the federation and the cantons.

2.2. Subsidiarity – the Role of the Cantons and the Communes

A crucial element of the Swiss political system is the principle of subsidiarity, which grants the communes and the cantons all powers that do not belong explicitly to the federal authorities.

---

[20] In German: *Konferenz der Kantonsregierungen* [author's note].

As has already been mentioned, Switzerland is a federal state consisting of three administrative levels: the federation, 26 cantons, and about 2850 communes. The decentralised division of the authorities' tasks and the tendency to carry them out on the lowest possible level, as dictated by the principle of subsidiarity, are the foundation of the state that has existed in a virtually unchanged form since 1848.

The Swiss federal state is a direct democracy in which the people hold the highest political authority, and citizens make laws through referenda. The universal nation-wide suffrage (both active and passive) was established in 1848 for men and in 1971 for women. Democracy, however, does not naturally invite everyone to take part in political life, and, sometimes, it may even exclude them from it. That was exactly the case in Switzerland: adult men often used their democratic privilege to deny voting rights to women. Since the 1880s, Swiss women had demanded the right to vote in an increasingly stronger manner. Men's opposition was unwavering and – under direct democracy – in full accordance with the law. This confirms the notion that democracy and progress do not always go hand in hand.

The crucial part of the current constitution of the Swiss Confederation is Article 3, which essentially determines the federal and the subsidiary character of the state: "The Cantons are sovereign except to the extent that their sovereignty is limited by the Federal

Constitution. They exercise all rights that are not vested in the Confederation."

It is just a one phrase, but it contains the whole essence of Swiss federalism and the principle of subsidiarity. All the more important is the interpretation of this article, which suggests that all of the state's institutions act within the law and in good faith, whereas their competencies are divided between the federal and the cantonal authorities. The former carry out only those tasks that are explicitly transferred to them by the constitution, and – since both levels of power mutually overlap – competence disputes are resolved through negotiations or mediation. The duties concerning the application of the federation's regulations are quite often transferred to the cantons, although it is not a rule. This decentralised federalism founded upon the principle of subsidiarity means that all decisions are made at the grass-roots level with the direct participation of citizens. The decisions that cannot be made on the communal level are made by cantonal authorities. In many areas, it is a rule that the federal government makes the law, but its implementation is left to the cantons, which do so according to their own requirements. **A strong federalist tradition compels the authorities of the individual cantons to focus on their own problems and to abstain from criticising the actions of the other cantons. It can be compared to a principle according to which competing companies do**

not criticise each other but carefully examine their methods. If a given method proves effective, every company sets out to implement it itself.

The cantons cannot be compared to the administrative regions, provinces, or districts in other democratic countries, e.g., voivodeships in Poland. They are essentially independent territorial units resembling states, with their own constitutions, and referring to themselves precisely as "states" (Ger. *Staat*, Fr. *Etat*). The cantons have virtually all the powers of a state, except for those that they voluntarily ceded in favour of the federation, such as defence and foreign policy. According to the general political doctrine of Switzerland, apart from observing their own, sovereignly enacted laws, the cantons are obliged to implement the general federal laws. As a result, the Swiss state has an exceptionally low number of conflicting or mutually obstructing regulations that are in force on the federal, cantonal, and communal level simultaneously.

After transferring certain competencies in favour of the federation, the cantons' numerous freedoms from before 1848 were significantly limited. However, despite the fact that the federation was gaining an increasing number of powers, the cantons did retain their strong position. It should not be forgotten that a major part of the federal revenues is distributed among the cantons. In the early days of the Swiss state's existence, the confederation's and the cantons' budgets were clearly separated. Every canton was obliged to carry out its duties with its own funds. The cantons did not receive any funds from the federation even for the realisation of the federal tasks and had to rely solely on their own tax revenues. Currently, the federation is obliged to share a part of its revenue with the cantons.

This results directly from the nature of the Swiss tax system, which is considered as one of the most complex in the world. Another cause is the diversity of the tax rates in different parts of the country and the cantons. Switzerland has three types of the income tax, which stems from the principle of subsidiarity: the communal, the cantonal, and the federal. Every Swiss canton and commune sets its own rate of cantonal and communal income tax. Each canton and each commune has is own tax act, which determines their revenues and assets. The system fosters competition between the cantons and the communes who try to attract companies and wealthy citizens with better tax rates.

The most important factor of the cantonal autonomy is that the cantons can adopt their own constitution, provided that it is in accordance with the provisions of the Federal Constitution, and that it strengthens the unity of the federation.

It is worthwhile to mention the basic political and legal factors that ensure the cantons' autonomy:

First, the existence of the cantons is guaranteed by the constitution. The federal legislators cannot create or dissolve any canton against its will. It is guaranteed by Article 53 of the Federal Constitution. In order to change the number of the cantons, or even to modify their territory, consent is required on the part of the community concerned, which means a long and complex procedure, including a cantonal referendum.

Second, the cantons organise their political life autonomously. Each establishes its own authorities, distributes competencies among them and determines rights, as well as duties, of its citizens. The federal law imposes only several basic principles that essentially come down to the ideas of equality and democracy. Apart from those principles, the cantons have absolute freedom in organising their internal political life.

Third, the cantons are free to elect their authorities. The Federal Council does not impose or suggest any candidates to the cantons and does not take part in elections of deputies or members of cantonal parliaments. It also lacks any powers to dissolve a canton's parliament or dismiss its government.

Fourth, the cantons are not subject to the Federation's political control. The cantonal constitutions require the approval of the Federal Assembly. The Federal Council monitors only certain cantonal laws. The majority of judicial decisions and rulings can be appealed before the Federal Supreme Court. These supervisions, however, differ from those of unitary states in that they are limited to the matter of legality, and not the jurisdiction. The Federal Council can, for example, refuse to accept a given law only when it decides that it violates the federal regulations.

The cantonal governments function as regulatory authorities in relation to the communes, while legislative power is vested in the cantonal council, i.e., the parliament, that usually consists of 100 councillors. The council is elected by the citizens of a given canton in general elections every four years. The cantonal parliament approves the budget, and passes the bills proposed by the government. It also appoints the highest cantonal officials and supervises important financial operations.

When analysing the Swiss political system, special emphasis should be put on the significant role of the communes, which constitute the foundation of the state. The rural and urban communes have retained their rights to this day, and their sovereignty is guaranteed by the constitution. A characteristic feature of the communes' organisation is their structural similarity, determined by their constitutions, which is an uncommon solution in other countries. A communal assembly consists of all citizens eligible to vote. Depending on the organisational system adopted in a given canton, the assembly exercises legislative power or appoints a representative authority with such power.

Communal autonomy is further confirmed by certain privileges, such as the right to levy taxes in order to fulfil communal needs or the freedom to act in matters outside the scope of the cantonal and federal competencies. In order to obtain the Swiss citizenship, it is necessary to first obtain a communal citizenship.

As Zdzisław Czeszejko-Sochacki describes in his monograph, these principles constitute the so-called core of the communal autonomy.[21] It should be remembered that it was **the communes that, throughout the centuries, were the embodiment of grass-roots democracy in Switzerland**.

Switzerland's subsidiary federalism is certainly a complex and costly system. In practice, however, it enables citizens to take a real and authentic part in the state's political life. It gives the individuals eligible to vote the satisfaction of deciding jointly about matters that concern them directly. Of course, the disputes and mediations between the specific levels of federal authority occur on a daily basis. An example of that is the problem of accommodating the immigrants who have come to Switzerland. The decision to admit them are made by the federal authorities. However, they are placed, naturally, on the territory of specific cantons. Some cantons oppose, while others agree without putting forward any additional conditions. This gives rise to the problem of financing the immigrants' residency. Some cantons demand support from the federation since they lack the means to provide for the masses of newcomers.

Local and political affiliation is deeply rooted in the mind of a Swiss citizen, who, primarily,

---

[21] Z. Czeszejko-Sochacki, *System konstytucyjny Szwajcarii*, Warszawa, Wydawnictwo Sejmowe 2002, p. 39.

identifies strongly with the commune and the canton and, only later, with the federation. A typical Swiss considers a different canton as a "foreign country," and people very reluctantly move from one canton to another.

2.3. The Party System and the "Magic Formula"

2.3.1. Political Parties

Usually, a political system includes parties and political institutions, as well as organisations and people who specialise in the field of politics.

The political system of Switzerland comprises all actors who take part in political decision-making.[22] In other words, all of the population who is eligible to vote is part of the political system of the country; aside from supporting the political parties, citizens take action through voting in referenda or engaging in popular initiatives.[23] If compared to other countries, the Swiss party system seems rather weak, which manifests itself in a significant internal division of

---

[22] A political system is the total of government agencies, political parties, organisations, and social groups (both formal and informal) that take part in political activities of a given country, as well as general principles and rules that regulate their interactions [author's note].

[23] M. Matyja, *Dysfunkcjonalność szwajcarskiej demokracji bezpośredniej*, Adam Marszalek, Toruń 2016, p. 71f.

each party. The structure of the system is determined by social and cultural divisions and – on the other hand – by the institution of federalism and direct democracy.[24] The fragmentation of the party system results from the high numbers of existing parties and the variability of its structure at the lowest federal levels. The configuration of the parties changes across the different levels of the local political system, i.e., it is different depending on the canton or the commune. It is typical that the structure of the party system on the cantonal or communal level is more coherent than on the federal tier. The significance of a given party is determined by two factors: whether it is able to enter a government coalition, and, if not, whether it is able to efficiently veto the government's decisions. These criteria result in the fact that there are only four significant political parties in Switzerland:

- Social Democratic Party of Switzerland (*Sozialdemokratische Partei der Schweitz*);
- Swiss People's Party (*Schweizerische Volkspartei*);
- Swiss Radical Democratic Party (*Freisinning-Demokratische Partei de Schweiz*);
- Christian Democratic People's Party (*Christlich-Demokratische Volkspartei der Schweiz*).

---

[24] Cf. W. Sokół, *System partyjny współczesnej Szwajcarii*, Annales UMCS, vol. V, 1998, p. 45–56.

Apart from these, there is also a plethora of minor parties:

Green Party of Switzerland (*Grüne Partei der Schweiz*), Liberal Party of Switzerland (*Liberale Partei der Schweiz*), Swiss Democrats (*Schweizer Demokraten*), Evangelical People's Party (*Evangelische Volkspartei der Schweiz*), conservative Federal Democratic Union (*Eidgenössische Demokratische Union*), communist Swiss Party of Labour (*Partei der Arbeit der Schweiz*), Ticino League (*Lega dei Ticinese*), conservative Freedom Party of Switzerland (*Freiheitspartei der Schweiz*), environmental-socialist Alternative List (*Alternative List*), (*Solidarités*) and progressive Christian Social Party (*Christlich-Soziale Partei*).

There is a different set of parties in every canton. Moreover, each party is internally divided when it comes to members' political views and agenda. The reason for this, among others, is the electoral system that undermines the party discipline. Due to the fact that votes are primarily cast for individual candidates (i.e., the individual with the highest number of votes is elected to the parliament, and not the one from the top of the list), and only secondarily for a party-list, the candidates are aware that they have been elected solely on the basis of their personal qualities. Whether voters trust a given party is merely a secondary matter. Parties often come to mutual agreements in order to put forward a number of candidates equal to the number of mandates. In such a situation, the cantonal government declares those candidates as elected, and elections are not called.

If there is a lasting government coalition, the minor parties usually have no influence on the state's politics. The opposition to the government is society itself; it expresses its voice through referenda, i.e., the most important instrument of direct democracy.

2.3.2. The Magic Formula

An essential characteristic of the Swiss party system is the cooperation of the major political parties in the Federal Council. The process is based on the so-called 'friendly agreement,' according to which the Swiss government comprises of many parties, but there are no coalitions, as it is, for instance, in Poland. Therefore, Switzerland lacks a typical parliamentary opposition. The process of forming the government had usually followed the so-called magic formula until 2003.[25] Between 1959 and 2003, the seven-member cabinet used to be formed according to the formula's non-written and non-formal rules:

- each of the parties with the best results in the elections appointed two members of the Council;
- the Italian- and French-speaking cantons appointed two members each;

---

[25] The magic formula is also known as "the golden seven" (Ger. *Zauberformel*) [author's note].

- the cantons of Bern, Zurich, and Vaud had to be represented as well;
- none of the cantons could have more than one representative.

Today, after many years, the Federal Council again comprises of the representatives of the four major parties.[26] However, a new algorithm for the magic formula has been negotiated due to the new political parties that have been represented in the government recently. To sum up, the result of the magic formula was, that between 1959 and 2003, regardless of the elections' results, power had been held (and is held again today) by essentially four major parties that represented nearly 70 percent of society: the Social Democratic Party of Switzerland (SP), the Liberal Democratic Party of Switzerland (FDP), the Christian Democratic People's Party (CVP), and the Swiss People's Party (SVP).

Such a division in the executive branch means that the government comprises of representatives of various political and cultural factions, as well as certain interest groups. This results in a high probability of reaching a compromise in which the needs of all the major political actors are taken into account. The

---

[26] In 2003, there was a split in the Swiss People's Party (SVP) that resulted in creation of the Swiss Bourgeois Democratic Party whose representative in the Federal Council was Eveline Widmer-Schlumpf [author's note].

main factor that, to some extent, compels the parties to cooperate and to share the offices in the Federal Council in line with the magic formula's rules has been the elimination of the risk of a non-obligatory (facultative) referendum, which may result in rejecting a law enacted by the Federal Assembly. This cooperation also decreases the risk of initiating a popular initiative in a situation of social dissatisfaction with the government's decisions.

Some authors wrongly suggest that the members of the Federal Council are typical public servants. Despite them being "flesh and bone" politicians, the Swiss government has no place for charismatic characters. It stems partially from the aforementioned magic formula, which imposes so many fundamental requirements on a politician (in terms of party, cantonal, and linguistic affiliation) that charisma, as a quality, loses its significance.

2.4. The Main Political Institutions

2.4.1. The Parliament

As it has already been mentioned, the state's legislative power lies in the hands of the bicameral parliament called the Federal Assembly, elected for a term of four years. The parliament comprises of the National Council (the smaller chamber) and the Council of States (the larger chamber). Similarly to other countries, it functions as the legislature by passing bills and amendments to the constitution.

The National Council is composed of 200 representatives elected in general elections based on a system of proportional representation. The cantons are the constituencies from which representatives are elected to the National Council. The number of deputies per canton is – in accordance to the principle of electoral equality – proportional to its population.

The Council of States comprises 46 members elected by cantonal legislative assemblies for a term of one to four years. Each canton elects two representatives to the larger chamber, while a half-canton elects one representative. The elections are based on the majority rule and a two-round system (an absolute majority is required in the first round and a simple majority in the second round).

Both chambers have equal rights, and both may initiate legislative procedures or supervisory actions. On the other hand, every legal act has to be approved by the two chambers. Thus, a bill does not become law if it is not passed both by the smaller and the larger chamber. A bill is always a result of compromise between the chambers. Each chamber is chaired by the president, elected for a term of one year without the possibility to be re-elected. The president, aided by two vice-presidents, chairs the sessions of a given chamber. When a tied vote occurs in any chamber, the president's vote is decisive.

The parliament elects the Federal Council (the government), the Federal Supreme Court (for a term of five years), the Federal President from among the members of the Federal Council (despite it being a rotary function, it has to be approved by the parliament) and a general Commander of the army in case of a direct national threat. Among the supervisory functions of the Federal Assembly is the overview of the government's and the Federal Supreme Court's activity, as well as the adoption of the government's budget. The parliament also supervises the cantons, takes measures to safeguard external and internal security, and ratifies international treaties and agreements. Switzerland lacks the classical separation of powers into legislative, executive and judiciary branches that should be characterised by equality and mutual supervision. The parliament is the supreme elective power to which the executive and the judiciary are subjected to. Therefore, the Swiss political system provides an advantage to the parliament, mainly through the rejection of the idea of a necessary organisational separation of powers. This stems from the multifaceted role of the parliament, which not only carries out the legislative, supervisory, and judicial tasks, but also manages and governs the state. Unlike other parliamentary systems, Switzerland lacks such parliamentary limitations as shortening the terms, summoning and closing the sessions by the executive, constitutional courts or judicial control of elections. The overview of the parliament is carried out by society – any law can be repealed at the request of 50,000 citizens eligible to vote through a non-obligatory referendum.

2.4.2. The Federal Council and the Federal President

In Switzerland, the Federal Council functions as the government. The Article 174 of the Federal Constitution of 1999 describes it as "the supreme governing and executive authority of the Confederation." In practice, the Federal Council, consisting of 7 members, is more of a coordinator than a government when compared to those in other democratic countries. The Council is elected by the Federal Assembly for a term of four years. The process of determining its composition follows the abovementioned magic formula.

The Federal Council is a collective agency, which means that any binding decision has to be made at a session with all members present. Voting always is preceded by a discussion. Such a method stems from the principle of equality of the ministerial offices – the ministers take decisions jointly. The collective nature of the Council means that its members are not personally responsible for the decisions. Some people maliciously say that actors earn more than the Swiss ministers because the latter do not play any role. Since all political parties – with their local organisations – are able to collect 50,000 signatures on a request for a non-obligatory referendum concerning any law, the decisions made by the Federal Council have to be reached through a compromise between all political factions. The magic formula virtually eliminates the division of the parliament into majority and opposition. Bills are drafted as a result of an agreement between all political forces.

Due to the multitude of its duties, the parliament forms federal departments (ministries in other countries), which are headed by the members of the Federal Council.[27] The departments' activity is supervised and criticised by the parliament, or, more precisely, by its supervisory committees. It is an essential factor that the heads of the departments cannot be dismissed by parliament. Parliament has the right to set tasks for the Federal Council through resolutions and postulates. A resolution may be issued by any chamber, although the other has to approve it anyway. Such a document obliges the Federal Council to submit a draft of a federal bill or to issue a binding recommendation. It is necessary for the government to examine a particular case and to submit a report containing a plan of further actions.

---

[27] There are the following departments in Switzerland: Federal Department of Foreign Affairs, Federal Department of Home Affairs, Federal Department of Justice and Police, Federal Department of Finance, Federal Department of Economic Affairs, Education and Research, Federal Department of Environment, Transport, Energy and Communications, Federal Department of Defence, Civil Protection and Sports [author's note].

The constitution does not provide for the office of the prime minister. The functioning of the government is based on the principle of joint authority and cooperation in decision-making. Its tasks consist of the overview of foreign policy, including the question of neutrality, internal affairs, and security, which includes the command of the federal army. The administrative matters comprise the overview of the activity of all federal public officials. This involves such tasks as the execution of the constitutional provisions, as well as the application of acts and resolutions of the parliament. The Council also has legislative (e.g., issuing executive orders, provided that the agency is authorised to do that by the constitution or an appropriate law) and supervisory competencies in relation to the cantonal authorities.

The Federal Council's position is further strengthened by the fact that it does not function as a typical government since it is not politically liable to the parliament. When it comes to its supervisory role, the Swiss parliament is limited to merely a control and criticism of the government and its activities. The Swiss political system lacks the instrument of the vote of censure on the government. The non-existence of the political responsibility on the part of the Federal Council is justified on the grounds of the system based on the principle of cooperation and consensus between the political parties represented in the government.

The members of the Federal Council decide between themselves about their dismissal or retirement, which, naturally, has its disadvantages. Usually, they resign from their ministerial office when they sense that they have lost their political party's support.

Every year, the Federal Assembly of the Swiss Confederation elects the president from among the members of the Federal Council, and the person elected retains the membership in the Council. The institution of the federal president lacks political significance. A minister who serves as the president still heads their department. The federal president is not the head of state, and does not function as the prime minister, although the federal president does head the Federal Council. A federal vice-president is elected from among the members of the Council and has virtually no competencies apart from substituting for the president in case of indisposition.

The competencies of the federal president include conducting the works of the Council and preliminary examination of issues presented by particular departments. The most important function is to represent the Swiss state abroad. Due to the fact that the federal president is elected every year and plays no significant role in the state's decision-making, citizens often do not know who the current president is.

Some authors and political scientists erroneously compare the position of the federal president in Switzerland to the position of presidents in other countries; the error stems from the fact that they ignore the term "federal," which explicitly points to the president's role as the head of the Federal Council and not the head of state.

2.4.3. The Federal Supreme Court

Located in Lausanne, the Supreme Federal Court is the chief judicial authority in Switzerland.[28] It was mentioned for the first time as an autonomous agency in the Swiss constitution of 1874. As the highest echelon in the federation, it decides on matters of criminal, civil, administrative and constitutional law; it also ensures uniform applications of law in individual cantons. The autonomy of the Federal Supreme Court is expressed in its function as an administrative agency that oversees the federal courts: the Federal Criminal Court, the Federal Administrative Court, and the Federal Patent Court.[29]

The characteristic feature of the Supreme Federal Court is that it examines citizens' complaints concerning the violation of their constitutional rights by laws issued by cantonal authorities. The procedure is quite common. In this way, citizens directly control and modify the laws of the federation.

---

[28] *Cf.* Article 188, Section 1 of the Federal Constitution.

[29] *Ibidem.*

2.5. Summary of the Second Chapter

The main feature of the Swiss political system is the threefold federalism combined with the principle of subsidiarity that permeates the constitution. Even though the principle itself lacks clarity, the parliamentary debate over a new constitution still revolves around it: both in regard to relations between the state and its citizens, and between the federation and the cantons. The principle is founded upon the ideas of helpfulness, responsibility and the mutual interdependence of citizens, which transcend the three administrative levels of the state. However, essentially, the principle states that specific matters should be resolved on a level that allows for the most efficient solutions. Equally important is the principle of cooperation between the cantons and the federal institutions. The crucial element of the Swiss political system that stems from the principles of federalism is a considerable independence and autonomy of the cantons and the communes. Although each canton has its own constitution, government and parliament, the cantonal law has to be in accordance with the federal law. It should be emphasised that the cantons constituting the Swiss Confederation have many powers typical of sovereign states.

The federal constitution of Switzerland allows the federal agencies to issue general directives, but making of the particular regulations lies in the hands of the 26 cantons, which gives them a wide range of possibilities to shape their own policy. The federation deals essentially with those matters that require uniform regulations for the whole country. Other matters are resolved by the cantons and the communes. In other words, the political power in Switzerland is centralised as far as it is necessary, and decentralised as much as it is possible. The central authority may impose a uniform law only if it had been previously approved by the majority of citizens and the cantons through an obligatory referendum.

The Federal Assembly (the parliament) is the highest authority in Switzerland. It is superior in regard to the other state agencies that it appoints, directs, and oversees. They lack the possibility to hinder its actions or to even oppose it.

The Federal Council, an executive agency, is elected according to the so-called magic formula, which states that government should comprise the representation of the major political parties, the largest cantons, and the largest linguistic groups.

3. The Characteristics of Direct Democracy in Switzerland

3.1. The Origins and Evolution of the Swiss Direct Democracy

3.1.1. The Period Before 1848

The political structure of Switzerland – i.e., the state agencies, the authorities, and forces (e.g., political parties) that take part in making and implementing political decisions, as well as methods and procedures used in this process – reflects the social system of the Swiss nation. The nation whose existence is based on the political will of its citizens. The Swiss national identity, in the form of, common among all citizens, feeling different from other nations, constitutes its political identity. All political and social institutions were established precisely for the maintenance of this identity.

The characteristic features of the Swiss three-levelled political structure are rooted in history. The division into the communes, cantons and the federation that binds them, is the product of Switzerland's past. The foundations of this structure are the communes, which, at first, were unions of land and farm owners, governed at the grass-roots level by their citizens. These unions were created in order to jointly solve problems related to owning land. With time, they started to deal with other issues that concerned the whole community, such as the maintenance of roads, transportation, tariffs etc. In this way, they transformed into public political associations.

The second level, and a very important element of the political system of Switzerland, are the cantons, which comprise of the communes combined into districts. According to the historian Stanisław Grodziski, during the era of the 1291 pact, it was the free peasant communes that were called the cantons.[30]

The first attempts at creating something resembling a state, a confederation of the cantons, date back to 1291 when the alliance was made between the representatives of the cantons of Uri, Schwyz, and Unterwalden. The pact concerned only matters of defence since, certainly, no one in the 13thC. thought yet about creating a Swiss sate. However, the pact also regulated the relations between its signatories. Interestingly, it was less significant for the inhabitants of the Swiss lands in 1291, than it is commonly assumed today. As a matter of fact, the document was quickly forgotten, and unearthed only in the

---

[30] S. Grodziski, *Porównawcza historia ustrojów państwowych*, UNIVERSITAS, Kraków 1998, p. 159.

18[th]C. According to the historian Guy P. Martial, it is important to emphasise that the pact was made by the communities whose representatives were deeply aware of their own independence. The making of the pact was followed by other arrangements between the independent communes.

With time, all of those arrangements and agreements between the communes or the cantons gained a defensive character and did not aim at creating a Swiss state, but, rather, a confederation, i.e., a loose union of free cantons. All cantons, cities and communes retained their privileges, and were able to determine their internal and foreign policy with full sovereignty. They also autonomously introduced tariffs and imposed taxes. The cantons maintained their independence and all essential elements of their political systems. The so-called *Landsgemeinde* played an important role in the political life of many communes, which were the assemblies of all adult men fit for military duty. They made crucial decisions concerning the communes, but, above all, they dealt with economic issues. After some time, they took up political issues as well. The power in the cantons belonged to the people's assemblies, i.e., to the representatives of the communes where they dwelled. The supreme authority, however, lay in the hands of the federal assembly of the cantons, which, nevertheless, was not a federal authority. In order to solve the cantons' problems, each of them sent delegates to annual sessions. In 1415, the city of Baden became the permanent place of these sessions. The assemblies followed the principle of unanimity, which meant that the federal assembly could not impose upon cantons any laws enacted by a majority of votes. During the sessions, the delegates strove to reach a compromise. Since the assemblies had no executive agencies, laws were implemented through appropriate decisions of the cantonal authorities and with the use of their own resources. The assemblies had powers in the areas of building and maintaining the roads, as well as ensuring security for the merchants who traded on the confederation's territory. The sessions also decided matters of defence and justice (both public and civil cases). However, the main task of the assemblies was the protection of independence, specifically from the Habsburgs, who continued to make claims on Swiss lands. The external threat was the chief factor in integrating the confederation, which, nevertheless, did not constitute a harmonious whole, but rather an arena of many internal conflicts. The cantons attempted to enlarge their territories through treatises and conquests, which led to inter-cantonal strife. Due to its expansionist politics, Zurich was especially active in provoking civil wars and endangering the unity of the confederation.

With time, two political factions evolved in Switzerland: liberals and radical democrats.

The former essentially agreed that the people are the sovereign, but they justified their model of democracy on the grounds of political immaturity and the incompetence of the ordinary citizen. **According to the liberals, a person without property and education is incapable of making common-sense political decisions aimed at the common good. On the other hand, the radical democrats claimed that the principle of the sovereignty of a nation does not mean that citizens should transfer their power to the elected representatives, but that the people should have the last word in decision-making**. According to the radical democrats, the model of direct democracy does not reflect common sense and common good in the best possible way. Nevertheless, they wanted to give all citizens equal powers in the political process and, thus, limit the influence of the liberal establishment.

3.1.2. The Development of the Modern Direct Democracy

The post-1848 Swiss direct democracy may be understood as a combination of completely new ideas and institutions with the old tradition of political participation (e.g., the communal assemblies). Democracy and liberty were no longer considered as the historical privilege of a particular group rooted in the resistance against tyranny – the tyranny fought against by William Tell.[31] From that time, **liberty and equality for all citizens** have become the leading motive of modern direct democracy. The previous form of Swiss democracy (before 1848) was perceived as the privilege of a particular group (the liberals) that enabled it in the oppression of other social groups.

Owing to the instruments introduced in 1848, citizens of Switzerland could, to a large extent, influence the authorities, their decisions, and the very process of governance. Swiss society gained the instruments that were to shape all levels of the country's political system. They included: the referendum, the popular initiative, the popular veto, the popular

---

[31] William Tell, a marksman with a crossbow, is a legendary Swiss national hero. According to tradition, William Tell refused to bow down before a symbol of an imperial power, for which he was punished by an Austrian reeve, Hermann Gessler. Gessler raised a pole in the market square of Altdorf (the capital of the canton of Uri), and placed his hat atop it. The citizens were ordered to bow to it. William Tell refused, was captured, and taken to face the reeve, who, having heard about the crossbowman's fame, came up with an idea: Tell was to shoot an apple placed atop of the head of his son, Walter. If he missed, both were to be executed. However, he passed the trial. When asked why there were two arrows in his quiver, he answered that if he had hit his son with the first one, he would have killed the reeve with the other. For intending to kill Gessler, Tell was sentenced to life imprisonment in Küssnacht dungeon. While being transported by a boat on Lake Urnersee, Tell escaped. Soon after, he killed Gessler, and by doing so he gave the signal that initiated the uprising which led to the cantons gaining independence from the imperial power, allied at the Rütli meadow. According to tradition, these events took place in 1307 [author's note].

consultation and popular assemblies in different parts of the country.

Two building factors of the post-1848 Swiss direct democracy should be pointed out: the ideas of the French revolution and the Swiss tradition of people's assemblies. The French revolution introduced the principles of the law-governed state – mainly, the threefold division of power – whereas the experiences of governing a commune shaped the Swiss direct democracy, grounded on referenda.

It should also be emphasised that the attainment of the modern form of the Swiss direct democracy was a gradual process that was initiated at the level of the communes and the cantons, and only later adapted to the federal level.

The first stage of the institutionalisation of direct democracy in the cantons occurred in the 1830s and was characterised by popular reforms carefully introduced by the liberals under significant pressure from the peasantry and radical democrats. Nevertheless, the principle of the parliament's supremacy was still dominant. The second stage occurred in the mid-19thC. and was directly connected with the introduction of the obligatory and the non-obligatory legislative referendum in the majority of the cantons. The third stage was the period just after the establishment of the federation. Especially in the 1860's, a growing number of cantons demanded the abolishment of the right to veto acts and the introduction of the obligatory and non-obligatory referenda, as well as the popular initiative.

The situation on the federal level was quite different. Here, the legal solutions concerning the institution of direct democracy were constitutionally guaranteed in 1848. It was then that the obligatory constitutional referendum and the popular initiative regarding a complete revision of the constitution were introduced. The extension of the institution of direct democracy occurred as a result of a full amendment of the constitution in 1874 by the introduction of the non-obligatory legislative referendum. Though, the possibility of proposing amendments to the constitution by citizens through the popular initiative was introduced in 1891.

Further changes extended the scope of the obligatory referendum to the matters of urgent regulations which have no constitutional basis (1949) and membership in international organisations (1977).

3.2. The Instruments of Direct Democracy in Switzerland

The idea of citizens' participation in political decision-making is an essential part of Switzerland's history. The state is governed by the people with the use of the instruments of direct democracy. The most prominent of them are: the popular (people's) initiative and referenda held at all levels of the political system – the communal, cantonal, and federal (Table 1).

Table 1. The forms of direct democracy in Switzerland (the federation, the cantons, and the communes).

The Federation	The Cantons	The Communes
Mandatory referendum	Mandatory referendum	Mandatory referendum
Optional referendum	Optional referendum	Optional referendum
Popular initiative (counter-project)	Popular initiative	Popular initiative
	Popular assembly	Individual initiative
		Local assembly

Source: M. Musiał-Karg, *Elektroniczne referendum w Szwajcarii. Wybrane kierunki zmian helweckiej demokracji bezpośredniej*, WNPiD UAM, Poznań 2012, p. 154.

Owing to these instruments, the nation has become a true sovereign – a subject holding an independent, superior authority. Each adult Swiss may decide on any important matter, from issues on the communal level to amending the federal constitution. This system of power, with such an enormous influence of interest groups and citizens on the decision-making, has no equivalent in any other modern country.

Switzerland has vast experience when it comes to direct democracy due to the frequent and common use of its instruments (Table 2).

Table 2. The use of the institutions of direct democracy in Switzerland between the years 1840 and 2014.

Period	Voting in general	Acceptance	Rejection	Popular initiatives		Mandatory referenda		Optional referenda	
				Yes	No	Yes	No	Yes	No
1840–1899	55	22	33	1	3	13	13	8	17
1900–1949	88	42	46	6	27	24	4	12	15
1950–1999	298	149	149	5	86	96	27	48	36
2000–2014	121	52	69	10	56	12	4	30	9
Total	562	265	297	22	172	145	48	98	77

Source: Own work based on: Center for Research on Direct Democracy, http://www.c2d.ch/inner.php?table=country_information&sublinkname=-country_information&countrygeo=1&level=1&menuname=menu&continen-t=Europe, accessed 20 August 2018.

In the years 1840 to 2014, the Swiss used the instruments of direct democracy 562 times. Forty seven percent of the voting resulted in the acceptance of proposed solutions. The popular initiative was initiated 194 times. In 22 of them society voted "yes." However, it should be pointed out that the accepted initiatives constitute only 11 percent of the solutions suggested by society. The contribution of this instrument to the changes proposed by citizens is rather minute. The referendum was used more often, as its efficiency is respectively larger than that of the popular initiative (Table 2).

3.2.1. Referendum

Referendum is a fundamental instrument of direct democracy. Shaped throughout the centuries, it enables citizens to decide on public matters. It is most commonly used on the communal level and, less so, on the cantonal and federal levels. As an expression of the society's voice, a referendum binds the authorities legally and produces legal effects in regard to the subject put to the vote.

There are two kinds of referenda in Switzerland: the mandatory (obligatory) and the optional (non-obligatory). According to Article 140 of the Constitution, there are three groups of issues that may be the subject of the mandatory referendum at the federal level:

- amendments to the Federal Constitution;
- accession to organisations for collective security or to supranational communities;
- emergency federal acts that are not based on a provision of the Constitution and whose term of validity exceeds one year (such federal acts must be put to the vote within one year of being passed by the Federal Assembly).[32]

In order to vote through a given proposal submitted to the referendum, it has to be accepted by the majority of society and the majority of the cantons. The optional referendum, also known as the popular

---

[32] See Appendix II.

veto, was introduced in 1874. It is implemented at the request of 50,000 citizens demanding to express their opposition to previously accepted solutions. The instrument is used against already enacted federal laws and international agreements. According to Article 142 of the Swiss constitution, the proposals submitted to the vote of the people become binding after being approved by a majority of voters.

For example, in the years 2000 to 2014 there were 55 referenda held, both mandatory and optional. Forty-two resulted in the acceptance of the proposed changes, whereas 13 resulted in rejections (Table 3).

Table 3. Referenda in the Swiss Confederation (as for 28 September 2014).

Period	Total	Mandatory referenda		Optional referenda	
		Yes	No	Yes	No
1840–1899	51	13	13	8	17
1900–1949	55	24	4	12	15
1950–1999	207	96	27	48	36
2000–2014	55	12	4	30	9

Source: Own work based on: Center for Research on Direct Democracy, http://www.c2d. ch/inner.php?table=country_information&sublinkname=-country_information&countr ygeo=1&level=1&menuname=menu&continen-t=Europe, accessed 22 August 2018.

As of today, all other countries combined have carried out only half as many referenda as the Swiss.

The referenda concern a wide spectrum of issues. To be more specific: the mandatory use of seatbelts (an optional referendum in 1980 – 51.6 percent voted *yes*), the accession to NATO (a mandatory referendum in 1986 – 75.7 percent voted *no*), mandatory maternal and sickness insurance (an optional referendum in 1987 – 57 percent voted *yes*).[33]

The most important referenda are those concerning the approval or rejection of a new constitution. In the history of the Swiss Confederation there were three constitutions adopted through a referendum: in 1848, 1874, and 1999. In 1972, on the other hand, a constitution was rejected in the same way. The current Federal Constitution of the Swiss Confederation was put to the vote on 18 April 1998. It was approved by 59.2 percent of the voters, 12 cantons, and 2 half-cantons. The majority of citizens decided that the main political principles contained in the document should come into effect and be the political basis of the Swiss Confederation. Eight months later, the constitution was passed by the Federal Assembly. The rejection by referendum of the idea of accessing the European Economic Area in 1992 was crucial for citizens' influence on the politics and the system of the Swiss Confederation. Eugeniusz Zieliński writes in his book, *Referendum w państwach Europy*, "Since the Second World War, no other decision has had such a great significance for Switzerland."[34] Altogether,

---

[33] W. Linder, *Demokracja szwajcarska*, Rzeszów 1996, pp. 152–153.

[34] E. Zieliński (ed.), *Referendum w Państwach Europy*, ASPRA 2005, pp. 301–302.

throughout Switzerland's past, there were hundreds, and thousands at the local levels, of different referenda.

Many authors claim, mistakenly in my opinion, that the Swiss referenda can be easily copied and introduced into the political systems of other countries. It is not that simple since the development of this instrument in Switzerland took centuries and resulted in working out a specific "referendal practice." It is also often forgotten that referenda held in other countries usually have no legal or constitutional basis. Moreover, the Swiss society has grown up in the tradition of having referenda. From childhood, a Swiss is confronted with the ideal of a highly sophisticated civil attitude, understanding their country's rules because they had been approved through referenda. If there is a disagreement with any rule, a social campaign may be started to initiate a referendum in order to change it. The results of referenda often surprise international observers. One of the many examples was the voting concerning the introduction of the public health insurance in 2012. It was supposed to be introduced alongside the already existing private one. Despite the appeals of the left, nearly 62 percent of the voters expressed themselves in favour of maintaining the completely private system. Claims that the health insurance contributions would increase were of no avail. The Swiss proved that what matters to them the most is the high quality of health care, which is considered as one of the best – and one of the most expensive – in the world.

3.2.2. Popular Initiative

The second instrument of the Swiss direct democracy is the popular initiative, defined by Articles 138 and 139 of the Constitution of 1999 (Appendix II). The subject of the initiative may be a total or partial revision of the Federal Constitution, proposed by 100,000 citizens eligible to vote, who have 18 months to collect the required signatures. They may request amendments or the abolishment of already existing regulations, or even propose new solutions.

The initiative may concern both particular and general solutions. If a proposal is put forward, it is first discussed in the Federal Council and the Federal Assembly, which take a formal stance regarding the proposed solutions. They may come forward with other propositions or elaborate on the ones already discussed. Next, all initiatives, including counter-propositions, are assessed by society and the cantons through referenda. The popular initiative is approved when a majority of society and a majority of the cantons express themselves in favour of it.

It should be mentioned that if the Federal Assembly advises against the popular initiative's proposal, it may put forward its own counter-proposal. Then, the nation and the cantons take a unanimous vote on the initiative and the counter-project at the same time.

This procedure seems complex to foreigners, but to the Swiss, who are used to the grass-roots method of governing the country, it is a daily occurrence.

In the cantons, where the assembly of citizenry (popular assembly) still functions, any bill may be the subject of the popular initiative. Any citizen who is a member of the assembly may put forward a proposal. In the cantons with representational legislative agencies, only a certain number of citizens have the right to submit a popular initiative, which may concern only those matters that are reserved for the jurisdiction of general voting (election of authorities, budget, important expenditures, appointment of public officials).

Table 4. Popular initiative in the Swiss Confederation (as for 28 September 2014).

Period	Total	Popular initiative		Counter-project	
		Yes	No	Yes	No
1840–1899	4	1	3	0	0
1900–1949	41	6	27	6	2
1950–1999	112	5	86	13	8
2000–2014	76	10	56	4	6

Source: Own work based on: Center for Research on Direct Democracy, http://www.c2d.ch/inner.php?table=country_information&sublinkname=-country_in formation&countrygeo=1&level=1&menuname=menu&continen-t=Europe, accessed 22 September 2018.

The popular initiative enables citizens to raise an important issue or problem that the authorities do not notice. It also enables citizens to change appropriate regulations. It is important since the Swiss know what they need best, and what needs to be changed

– naturally, in accordance with applicable law. Through the popular initiative a citizen may get involved in many issues such as: taxes, finance, economy, army, farming, alcohol and tobacco, telecommunications, foreigners, education, nuclear energy, work, health care, environmental protection etc.

It is worthwhile to mention that every approved initiative ends with it being put to the vote in a referendum. If such an initiative is rejected, the problem which it concerns itself is made noticeable to the politicians and society. Usually, such initiatives are not ignored in the decision-making process: the authorities generally react in some way out of the fear of an alternative initiative.

3.2.3. Popular Assembly

The popular assembly, which – unlike the referenda and the popular initiative – is not mentioned in the Federal Constitution. It is an open-air gathering of citizens eligible to vote who assemble on a central square of a canton (*Landsgemeindeplatz*) in order to debate and decide about the most important cantonal issues. During those yearly assemblies, the people decide about, among other things, the cantonal expenditures,. Each participant of the *Landsgemeinde* may take the floor during the debate. Voting takes place through the raising of a hand and is treated as a mandatory referendum. It is possible to make the voting process confidential. Moreover, the subject of the assembly may be limited to the election of specific authorities or to putting it to the vote a matter without discussing it first. Due to practical reasons, *Landsgemeinde* has been done away with in all but two cantons where it is still the supreme political institution. Those exceptions are the cantons of Glarus and Appenzell Innerhoden.

In about 80 percent of the communes, there is the so-called citizens' assembly (the local meeting) – *Gemeindeversammlung* (also known as *Einwohnerversammlung*). During those meetings, anybody interested and eligible to vote may participate in deciding about the most important issues concerning the community. The meetings, which are essentially a copy of the cantonal *Landsgemeinde*, take place several times a year.

Landsgemeinde is undoubtedly the purest instrument of direct democracy, deceptively similar to voting in ancient Athens. Despite the fact that today it is obsolete, it is still very important to the traditional Swiss. It was a popular assembly that throughout the centuries was the only form of grass-roots democracy in Switzerland and the basis of its political system.

3.3. Summary of the Third Chapter

The fact that citizens have enormous influence over the political decision-making is the essence of the

Swiss political system. The crucial instruments of the system that have been developed throughout the centuries are: referenda and the popular initiative.

A referendum enables citizens to decide about the public issues. Its result not only constitutes a public expression of society's will, but also binds the authorities and produces legal effects regarding a particular matter. One hundred thousand citizens eligible to vote, who – through the popular initiative – have 18 months to gather the required signatures, may subject to a referendum any issue, leading to the amendment of the Federal Constitution.

4. The Debate About Direct Democracy in Switzerland

4.1. The Efficiency of Direct Democracy

It should be emphasised again that citizens' participation in power is the foundation of the efficient functioning of the Swiss state. The citizens who vote are considered sovereign. The decisions, however, are not taken by the people in general – as some of the media wrongly report – but by those eligible to vote, who constitute about 60 percent of the Swiss. The average attendance at polling booths fluctuates at around 40 percent. Therefore, the decisions are taken by about 25 percent of the population, i.e., less than 2 million citizens. The average majority required to vote through a given project is over 1 million citizens, i.e., 12–13 percent of the population. That is the percentage of the Swiss who approve or reject the propositions put forward by the authorities or through the popular initiative and decide on the most important matters. In the 1970's, there was a significant increase in the number of voters which resulted from granting women the right to vote in 1971. The percentage of the eligible to vote rose from 14% to 12–18%.[35] It means that the deciding majority of voters is made up of a minority of the population. This gives rise to the problem of how concurrent are the political views of those who vote and of those who do not participate in voting.

Given the fact that such a modest number of the Swiss possess such significant power, it can be provocatively stated that in this situation the parliament itself would seem sufficient as the exponent of the nation's will. However, it should be remembered that citizens' direct participation in the governance of a country, regardless of its degree, is always the most appropriate way of legitimising the state's power. The will of the nation is expressed by those who want to express it. Those who do not vote are not barred from participation. Despite the low percentage of active voters and the accusations of the tyranny of the majority (who, in fact, constitute a minority of the population), the main entity that shapes the political system of the Swiss Confederation is the people, or, more precisely, the electorate – not particular public authorities.

---

[35] Based on the author's calculations.

Based on the motivations that lie behind the decisions made through referenda, Wolf Linder distinguishes three groups of those eligible to vote:[36]

1. Those who vote with their "wallets." They vote *yes* or *no* depending on whether it benefits them individually.
2. Those who are motivated by the political ideas of the faction that they represent.
3. Those who vote with their "hearts." They vote according to the suggestions made by various authorities in the field of religion, tradition, social matters etc.

Linder points out that 30 percent of the eligible to vote are aware of their civil duties and vote regularly. About 20 percent are the so-called "teetotallers" who – due to various reasons – have never voted. The most numerous group that constitutes nearly 50 percent are, as Linder describes them, *a la carte* voters – they vote from time to time. Whether they will participate in a given voting depends on its subject.[37]

As has already been mentioned, essentially any issue put to the vote by citizens may initiate changes to the current agenda of the Swiss political process. Public authorities and politicians often remove problematic

---

[36] W. Linder, p. 147–148.

[37] *Ibidem*, p. 148.

issues from scheduled debates and deliberately ignore them. Their goal is to avoid any objections by society. On the other hand, the Swiss direct democracy enables citizens to raise questions and decide on matters that would never be set on the political agenda of other countries with parliamentary democracy. That is the aim of the already discussed instruments: the referenda and the popular initiative. Due to the "innovative" nature of the latter one, it allows the political agenda to extend with new issues. The low efficiency of the initiative does not lessen its importance; the very signalling of a particular problem through the initiative is already a highly significant factor.

The referendum, however, is a tool that provides control over the political system and enables society to express its will in a legally binding manner. Citizens may state their opinion by approving or rejecting a given solution through referenda. The most important issues are decided upon in the obligatory referendum. Whenever the constitution is to be changed, the political authorities have to consider the fact that any amendment may be rejected by the electorate. Therefore, public authorities formulate the text of an amendment in such a way so as to avoid a potential referendum. The threat of initiating a referendum is constant, which compels the authorities – due to the fear of complete rejection – to adjust the draft so that it becomes a compromise between their goals and society's voice. The authorities consult their decisions with society represented by interest groups, trade unions etc. The same procedures are used in the case of issues that are subject to the facultative referendum. This indicates that, as an instrument, referendum not only influences the power directly but also constitutes an indirect factor that shapes the political system. **The awareness of the power that society possesses through its political tools compels the authorities to respect its opinions**. An example of this is the debate on the purchase of new aircraft and missile defence systems for the Swiss army. The government is doing everything it can to avoid a referendum on this issue despite the fact that a withdrawal from such a purchase may have negative effects on Switzerland's defences.

Another feature of the Swiss referendum is its "vetoing" character. It is an essential tool for blocking the authorities' decisions. Society frequently opposes the federal or cantonal parliament's decisions and initiates a referendum in which it rejects a given idea or draft.

In constitutional matters, society does not have to initiate a referendum since, in this case, it is obligatory for the public authorities to hold a referendum each time an idea of changing the constitution arises.

It should be pointed out that it was direct democracy that led to the evolution of the Swiss political system. The institution of referendum strengthened the idea of joint governance by consolidating the

Swiss consensual democracy based on the principles of agreement and cooperation.[38] Because of this, a referendum can also be an efficient tool in the hands of small interest groups, who – while putting forward their own proposals – are able to gather the majority necessary to approve or reject a given draft. Interest groups are a very important factor that shapes the Swiss political system. Factions representing various parts of society compete for their ideas. They are, for instance, environmental groups and trade or labour unions. Referendum – or, more importantly, the very threat of initiating it – is a tool that lobbyists can use to influence the authorities. The mechanism is simple: "if we do not get what we want, we will initiate a referendum." Nevertheless, the popular consultation preceding a referendum still provides an opportunity for all groups to negotiate. It is a practical confirmation of the Swiss principle that "the winner does not get everything, and everybody wins something." It is very often visible whenever a compromise is reached between an interest group and the government that is fully aware of the power possessed by citizens and their formal and informal associations.

Direct democracy is extremely popular in Switzerland. Citizens know the potential of its

---

[38] Consensual democracy is a state in which power is divided between various institutions and levels of the political system. Since power is not concentrated in a single governing body, the majority is unable to make decisions that would harm the interests of minorities [author's note].

instruments. They use them whenever it is necessary, which distinguishes Switzerland from other democracies. Many political scientists, however, accuse it of lacking an innovative nature and an openness to the international community. For example, Switzerland only joined the United Nations – after a referendum – in 2002, i.e., 57 years after the establishment of the organisation that currently has over 190 members. Moreover, the Swiss state is far behind the current trends in international integration. As it has been already mentioned, progress does not always go hand in hand with democracy. The Swiss, however, say that they may be slow in their decision-making, but this slowness usually beneficial.

One has to admit that the Swiss system of direct democracy functions almost perfectly. Nobody blames others for making bad decisions since everyone can personally take part in the process. By not participating in voting, citizens harm only themselves. The Swiss humorously say that the worst decisions are taken by those who do not vote.

The equality and openness of citizens is exemplified by the fact that **everybody settles and pay their taxes themselves, which means that everybody knows how much and why they pay**. Naturally, everybody tries to minimise the rates, within permissible limits. Moreover, citizens know that they can initiate a political process that would aim at changing the tax rates. The experience of paying taxes incentivises citizens to demand budget statements from the communes, the cantons, and the federation. Apart from that, citizens of every commune have full access to each other's income statements, and the federal tax administration grants all citizens access to any information regarding personal and corporate income, wealth and property tax in Switzerland. Citizens may also find out how much communal civil servants earn, or how much the commune spent on culture, a new school etc. While all this data is available on demand, citizens often do not even have to ask for it since it has to be made public in order for a relevant project to be put to the vote in the popular initiative. For instance, before starting a construction of a new gymnastic hall in a commune, its plans have to be approved through voting, and an estimate of expenditures has to be published in the communal official gazette so as to allow for a potential civil protest. The earnings of the communal civil servants, including the communal president, as well as the parish priest, the local bank manager etc. are public. There are no payments for Masses, baptisms, weddings, or funerals etc. In order to pay for such services, the Swiss introduced the so-called "church tax." The church itself has to be listed on the official register of religious denominations.

There are numerous other examples. The goal here is to show that the system of direct democracy proves to be efficient and practical, although – as in

any political system – it has its advantages and disadvantages.

4.2. The Advantages of Direct Democracy

First, direct democracy makes it easier for citizens to participate in political decision-making. Even entities that are not part of the governmental structures may decide about the country's fate. It is also important that citizens consciously bear responsibility for the decisions they take at the polling booths.

Second, every political entity, even an individual citizen, is able to efficiently put forward its demands. Even the initiatives and referenda that have no chance of success in the first place, are undertaken. They still provide a contribution to the country's politics by indirectly influencing public opinion.

Third, direct democracy is characterised by a strong tendency for compromise and respect for public opinion. It means that politicians are in constant contact with society due to the fear of the initiation of the popular initiative. It provides an opportunity for minorities to force through their suggestions or demands.

Fourth, in a system of direct democracy all participants of the political, economic and social arena widely accept all political decisions. A decision made through a referendum is certainly more convincing for society than one that is made by a narrow political elite. This significantly eases social tensions and limits the influence of lobbyists since any draft made under their pressure may be rejected in a referendum.

Fifth, the fact that the Federal Council is made up of members of the political parties with the highest support level eliminates the phenomenon of them forming hostile factions (known in other countries as "the opposition"). As a result, there is no "appropriation" of the country by the winning majority.

Sixth, direct democracy plays two vital roles in the decision-making process: political communication and political socialisation. Through political communication – due to the vast number of political entities involved in the decision-making – it **fosters society's political knowledge, making it higher than in the systems based on representative democracy**. Moreover, it facilitates the tendency for compromise and creates an extensive network of political and social relations in which information is exchanged. Political socialisation means that the participation in the system of direct democracy consolidates the social awareness of the basic democratic rights, such as the respect for the arguments of one's political opponents. The factors of political socialisation include: family, school, social and occupational circles, as well as mass-media. In such a stable political system as the Swiss one, political socialisation guarantees its permanence on every level of society.

4.3. The Disadvantages of Direct Democracy

The disadvantages of direct democracy, just as its advantages, are a relative, complex, and multi-levelled problem.[39]

First, although the system enables wide participation of citizens in the political life of the country, only a small part of society is actively involved in the process. While this minority is comprised of those who vote, the remaining majority has to comply with its views and opinions. The attendance at polling booths confirms it: on average, only 40 percent of those eligible to vote take part in voting, and foreigners (who constitute 20 percent of society) are not allowed to be actively involved in the country's politics.

Second, direct democracy slows down political decision-making, which in turn inhibits and blocks the process of finding necessary solutions. Due to the large number of political actors involved (parties, interest groups, society as a whole), reaching a compromise is difficult and takes a lot of time. Naturally, it is debatable whether it is a systemic disadvantage or an advantage.

Third, direct democracy undermines the position of the established political actors since it creates an opportunity to omit the jurisdiction of particular government agencies. In this way, interest

---

[39] M. Matyja, *op. cit.*, p. 112n.

groups may bring up issues considered important from their own, self-interested, perspective without being held politically responsible. As a result, such groups stand between society and the state as competition for political parties, whose position is thereby undermined. The Swiss farmers' lobby is the best example of this.

Fourth, due to the multiplicity and diversity of the decisions taken by voters in direct democracy, society becomes passive. Voters cannot inform each other systematically about all occurring changes as the costs of exchanging information are too high, especially when it comes to decisions on complex issues. Only 1/6 of Swiss voters are fully informed the day before a referendum.

Fifth, the system of direct democracy may ignite political conflicts. It is particularly visible when voting concerns an "all or nothing" issue. Such cases increase the risk of escalating political animosities.[40]

Sixth, the dysfunctionality of the system of direct democracy is also visible in the process of implementing a solution approved in a referendum. It rarely occurs that the implemented solution exactly reflects the will of the society expressed at the polling booth. It is the parliament that decides how the implementation is carried out. It has to take into

---

[40] An example of this is the 2009 referendum on banning the construction of minarets [author's note].

account some additional aspects, such as international law and the constitutionality of the new solutions. As a result, the introduction of a new constitutional amendment or bill is often "watered down," i.e., it does not fully meet the expectations of the group that initiated it. This, naturally, brings disappointment and resentment. An example of this is the initiative concerning the expulsion of the so-called foreign criminals. Although parliament took a decision that introduced exemptions from this rule, which contradicted the proposed initiative, the passed regulations are in accordance with the federal constitution and international law.

The above-mentioned disadvantages of the Swiss direct democracy are not as serious and they cannot endanger the *raison d'ètat* of the Swiss state. Nevertheless, it is worthwhile to remember that, in spite of numerous praises from politicians and political scientists, even the Swiss political system has its flaws.

4.4. Summary of the Fourth Chapter

The most important and frequent arguments used to show Switzerland's direct democracy's flaws are:
1. that politics should be restricted only for competent individuals;
2. that direct democracy prolongs the decision-making process.

These arguments, however, do not seem convincing. Studies show that the level of competence among the eligible to vote is insignificant for the outcome of a referendum. It is nevertheless true that direct democracy makes the decision-making process longer, although it should be pointed out that acting in haste is not always good. It is often more important to discuss a problem thoroughly and substantially.

The direct democracy in Switzerland enables citizens to raise questions and decide on matters that in other circumstances would not be set on the **political authorities'** agenda at all.

The Swiss model of democracy, as any other political system, has its advantages and disadvantages. It seems, however, that the advantages outweigh the flaws, and the latter do not threaten the efficacy of the system's functionality.

5. Direct Democracy in European Countries

5.1. Support for direct democracy in Europe

In 2007, in order to allow its citizens to exercise their rights in the spirit of direct democracy, the EU introduced the instrument called the European Citizens' Initiative. By collecting a required number of signatures, ordinary people have the possibility to influence laws and policies. However, it should be noted that when the Initiative was created, many EU countries had already had their own similar mechanisms. Nevertheless, the scale and efficiency of how they are used differs significantly depending on the country, its administrative level, and the people's attitudes.

In 2017, the Pew Research Center polled ten EU countries in order to analyse the people's opinions on democracy[41]. The results showed that a median of 50 percent of citizens consider the functioning of democracy in their country as unsatisfying, while

---

[41] See: https://www.realclearworld.com/articles/2018/01/31/europeans_want_direct_democracy_112694.html (accesed: 27.11.2018).

48 percent stated the opposite. However, opinions vary significantly from country to country: 79 percent of Swedes, 77 percent of the Dutch, and 73 percent of Germans said that they are satisfied with their present democratic system. On the other hand, of the same opinion were only 25 of the Spanish and 21 percent of Greeks. It is worth mentioning that the numbers come from before the secessionist vote in Catalonia.

According to the poll, popular support for the present forms of democracy in Europe is far from convincing. Despite the fact that a median of 80 percent of those surveyed view representative democracy in a positive way, the level of that support is quite diverse. While 54 percent of Swedes are in favour of a system with elected representatives as the ones determining laws, only 20 percent of Poles have a similar attitude towards their parliamentary system.

However, when it comes to the long-term perspective, the data suggest that the main factor determining the shape of European democracy will be the Europeans' very desire to directly participate in the political process. This means that there is significant probability that the support for direct democracy will increase in the future.

The results of the poll partially illustrate this trend. For example, a median of 70 percent of the adults in Europe think that referendum is one of the most efficient tools of governance. Such opinion expressed eight-in-ten Greeks and three-quarters of the Spanish, Germans, and French. Interestingly, although the majority of citizens in the Netherlands (55 percent) and the United Kingdom (56 percent) support direct democracy – the two countries have organised national referenda quite recently – their approval is the lowest in Europe.

Direct democracy is particularly popular among the followers of certain populist parties. Eighty-eight percent of the Podemos party supporters in Spain believe that allowing citizens to vote on national matters would be beneficial for their country. Eighty-four percent of the Alternative for Germany (AfD) supporters in Germany and 77 percent of the Party for Freedom (PVV) supporters in the Netherlands are of the same opinion. This shows that less educated people are also able to see advantages of direct democracy.

Interestingly, it is the followers of the Eurosceptic parties that express particularly firm support for a popular vote on continued EU membership. In fact, some of them have called for referenda on this matter – in favour of doing it were 84 percent of the National Front supporters in France, 69 percent of AfD supporters in Germany, 69 percent of the PVV supporters in the Netherlands, and 63 percent of the Five Star Movement (M5S) supporters in Italy[42].

A median of 18 percent of the people polled in the nine continental EU member states were in

---

[42] Ibidem

favour of their country leaving the EU. Therefore, if the Europeans' demand for the introduction of more efficient tools of direct democracy into their countries' political systems is satisfied, Brexit may inspire other nations to take similar steps in the future.

Below is an analysis of the development of direct democracy in four different countries: the Netherlands, Austria, Slovenia, and Poland.

5.2. Austria

The constitution of Austria grants its citizens the right to put forward a petition to the parliament, provided that they collect the required number of signatures. Popular petition has proved to be an effective instrument in dealing with issues, such as nuclear and hydropower, school class sizes, reform of the state broadcaster, immigration policy, women's rights, genetically modified food, and post offices.

In the last 50 years there have been 33 popular petitions in Austria with over 11.5 million signatures collected (340,000 each on average). What is interesting, is that all of them were officially accepted. There was only one petition that did not manage to attract the required 100,000 signatures.

It is difficult to assess the real impact of this instrument on the Austrian policies. For instance, in 1985, citizens who opposed the construction of a hydropower dam on the Danube managed to collect 353,906 signatures. Such a vast support certainly had an influence on the government's decision to abandon its plans. Another result of this successful grass-roots campaign was the consolidation of the then newly formed Austrian Green Party, which still states direct democracy as one of its fundamental ideals.

At some point, petitions turned out to be one of the factors that determined the shape of the political right. Due to a campaign opposing immigration organised in 1993 (called "Austria First!"), Jörg Heider assured the leading position of the far right faction in the Freedom Party (FPÖ). This caused a split in the party, which was left by its more liberal members. In 2006, the current chairman of the FPÖ, Heinz-Christian Strache, initiated a petition in order to signal citizens' opposition to the Treaty of Lisbon and to call for a referendum on Turkey's accession to the EU – the project managed to attract 258,281 signatures. While their opponents on the left tend to focus on environmental matters and human rights, Austria's far right seems to be the first group to exploit the European Citizens' Initiative on a wider political scale.

It should be noted, however, that politicians are in no way in favour of being told what to do – even through such democratic tools as citizens' initiative. This dismissive attitude towards public opinion is exemplified by the 1997 petition to strengthen women's rights. Despite the 644,665 signatures collected and positive opinions by various politicians, nothing has been done in terms of the government's policy.

5.3. The Netherlands

The system of direct democracy in the Netherlands is exemplified by the so called citizens' initiative (*Burgerinitatief*). Through this tool Dutch voters can draw the parliament's attention to particular issues and start a political debate. Although the initiative does not immediately compel politicians to introduce or change any laws, its main effect is to make a given problem a matter of public discussion.

The requirement for starting a petition is that the interested citizens have to be of Dutch nationality and eligible to vote. In order to be formally valid, the proposal has to include their name, address and signature. The validity of the signatures is further verified at random by a special commission in the Hauge. If the proposal attracts at least 40,000 signatures, it is set on the parliament's agenda. Moreover, it is also possible to start an initiative at the local level. The minimal number of signatures required is much lower and varies from region to region (it can be a 100 or 1,000). Usually, signatures are collected *via* the Internet, in town centres or shopping malls.

Despite the accessibility of the mechanism, there have only been three parliamentary discussions started through the citizens' initiative that concerned:

- a ban on festive fireworks (60,000 signatures collected),
- a ban on smoking in all public places (around 60,000 signatures),
- a ban on selected intensive farming techniques, proposed by an environmental organisation (over 100,000 signatures).

All of these attempts were unsuccessful since in each case the parliament lacked a proper majority to back the proposals. The initiatives, however, did manage to attract a public attention to the problems they signalled.

When it comes to the practice of direct democracy on the lower administrative tier, the situation is very similar. Since the introduction of the citizens' initiative on the local level in 2002, 63 percent of the municipalities have not used it even once. It seems that the only attempts at starting an initiative have come from various influential lobby groups.

5.4. Slovenia

Despite having a population of 2 million, Slovenia has quite a large number of instruments of direct democracy. There is, however, a significant discrepancy between the functioning of the system at the local and the national level. Whereas it is easier to organise a referendum locally, it is not so at the national administrative tier where a failure to collect the required number of signatures is often the case. There are different requirements in terms of signatures for initiating different political processes:

- at least 5,000 signatures are required in order for citizens to propose a new law,
- at least 30,000 signatures are required in order to propose an amendment to the constitution,
- at least 40,000 signatures are required for citizens to demand a referendum.

Since regaining its independence, Slovenia has had over a dozen national referenda. Apart from that, there have been a number of local referenda initiated by citizens on setting up new communes and creating or closing landfill sites. On the other hand, many citizens' initiatives to hold a referendum were unsuccessful. An example of such a failed attempt was the joint project of a patriotic organisation called the 25 June Institute and the non-parliamentary Slovenian National Party (SNS). The groups, opposed to Croatia's accession to NATO, wanted a referendum on the issue. Eventually, the initiative did not go off since the groups managed to collect only a 1,000 signatures, while the parliament issued a positive opinion on Croatia's joining NATO.

When it comes to referenda at the local level, the turnout is usually high despite the fact that such initiatives are organised by small political movements or citizens' themselves. This is understandable since the issues raised, such as building a powerplant or a landfill site, concern them directly.

The popularity of local referenda does not, however, translate into the national level. Here, campaigns are mainly initiated by members of parliament. Slovenian public opinion, sceptical of its representatives, considers most of the initiatives as a violation of democratic principles and a misuse of public funds. Since many people see such projects as means of manipulation aimed at political gain of the interested parties, the turnouts are generally very low. The only two exceptions were the referenda on Slovenia's accession to the EU and NATO in 2003 when over a half of the eligible population cast their vote.

Summary of the Part I

The question whether the political system of Switzerland is efficient requires an ideological discussion since it cannot be directly compared to the systems of other countries. Its federalism, combined with direct democracy, has so many aspects that – depending on one's point of view – may be considered as both advantages and disadvantages.

Due to its multiculturalism, without relying on direct democracy it would be difficult for Switzerland to reach any socio-political compromise. The system ensures that the ethnic, linguistic or religious minorities do not feel harmed or discriminated. The fact that many decisions are made on the lowest administrative level protects citizens from the state's unjustified or misguided interventions.

In this way, direct democracy inhibits intercultural and ethnic tensions and adjusts the states' activity to the interregional differences. The scarcity of regional, local, and political conflicts is the best evidence that the Swiss federal state is efficient and thoroughly democratic. Although negotiations between the cantons, or between the cantons and the federation – a phenomenon usually obscure to other countries – often take a long time, yet, in the end, they can yield positive results.

The costs of the system are undoubtedly its major flaw. Each canton has its own government, administration, judiciary etc. Even the universities are funded by the cantons. The political system of Switzerland is not perfect, and it is not unique in this respect. However, given the internal and external situation of the country, the Swiss – despite the globalisation and the expansion of the European integration – would not want to have any other system. The cantonal competencies and the direct democracy are consistently protected, and whenever any inter-cantonal controversies arise, they are solved by peaceful agreements.

On the other hand, the lack of any essential division of power puts the principles of democracy up in the air. In practice, the system certainly does not guarantee transparent relations between the parliament and the government, which – due to the similar powers that these bodies possess – can mutually hamper their activities. The lack of political responsibility on the part of the government also can generate various problems. For instance, since there is no vote of censure on the government, it cannot be dismissed even if it is highly inefficient. As a result, the society has to endure it throughout its whole term. The expansion of direct democracy's procedures and frequent use of referenda provide the people with a unique influence on the form of the state's politics. It also discredits the parliament as the key democratic institution of political representation. The problems deepen even further when outcomes of referenda lack a proper legitimisation due to a low attendance at the polling booths.

The above discussion raises the following question: is the Swiss direct democracy functional at all? In answering it, we shall rely on a simplified, yet useful, model of the main choices and challenges that the Swiss political decision and strategy makers face. Based on theory and empirical observation, it is sensible to reject any hypothetical, extreme, "either-or" type of assessment of the Swiss system. It is so because, in practice, it is impossible to describe specific political decisions made within the framework of direct democracy as purely functional or dysfunctional. Their analysis should be complemented by a formula that can be colloquially named as "both this and that." For it is precisely this formula, marked by the Swiss attitude of compromise, that functions at the core of the Switzerland's decision-making. A similar approach should be applied to the advantages and disadvantages of the Swiss political system.

The growing external and internal pressures compel the Swiss to find a balance between them and to adjust to two interconnected phenomena: international cooperation on the one hand, and independence and neutrality on the other. In the modern globalised world, it is not an easy task for such a relatively small country as Switzerland. Nevertheless, the history of Switzerland and its political system shows that – especially when compared to other nations – the transfer of power into the hands of the actual sovereign, i.e., the country's citizens, has yielded positive results.

This raises another question: can other countries copy the instruments of the Swiss democracy? When it comes to referenda, it is certainly possible. The best example is the Brexit referendum in Great Britain. It should be, however, remembered that, in most countries, referenda are not legally binding. In the case of the popular initiative, and especially the popular assembly, it would be more difficult, as Switzerland, in regard to these instruments, has a vast and unique experience, gained throughout the centuries and in specific conditions. It is doubtful that these instruments would function well on *ad hoc* basis in other countries. Generally, direct democracy can function properly, specifically, in small countries like Switzerland. In the case of bigger countries, it is more difficult, hence the necessity of electing representatives from among society.

Apart from that, it is often forgotten that direct democracy is a very expensive system (although appearances can be deceptive). Being one of the richest countries in the world, Switzerland can afford this "democratic luxury." However, it is worth noticing that only 150 years ago Switzerland was a very poor country.

In the real world of politics, it is necessary to strive for a proper balance between one democratic way of developing a country and another; it is not easy. Such a balance changes over time and depends on the level of development and maturity of a given political system, as well as many internal and external factors. In the Switzerland's case, it boils down to defining the direction the political decision-making should follow, regardless of the existing types of democratic instruments. The Swiss system of direct democracy and the decisions taken by the electorate at the polling booths is the Swiss direction that the federal and the cantonal authorities are to follow. **It is worth stressing that the law made by the people for the people is certainly not a political utopia, but, rather, it provides opportunities for making optimal political decisions in particular circumstances.**

Part II

Direct Democracy in Poland

Introduction

Most Poles, when asked, agree that there is a need for change in their country's political system. Some of them ask further: "but how and when should it occur?"

What causes this common attitude?

One of the reasons may be the fact that the transformation from communism to a semi-democratic system that happened 30 years ago in such an abrupt manner was accompanied by selling off of the country's assets, economic scandals, failed Balcerowicz Plan, as well as seizing the power by corrupt elites. Sadly, the consequences of those events are felt to this day.

It is a common knowledge that during the '90s Poland was used as a testing ground for the project of the systemic transformation. Citizens were told that all financial transactions conducted in the process of privatization had to be classified. In this way, the people in power – promoted to their positions as a result of the Round Table Agreement in 1989 – sold off national assets, without explaining to the society who were the buyers and what was the price.

The "reformers" argued that there was no other method of improving the nation's existence; that the only possibility was a quick and full privatization of the national economy. Politicians, and the media, argued that the crisis could be resolved in one of the two ways: the communist one and the liberal one. The idea of liberalisation of the economy became the most popular slogan, palmed off on the disoriented and exhausted society.

The most important means of quick selling of the country's assets was the famous Balcerowicz Plan. Intended to last for about six months, it basically goes on to this day.

According to various unofficial estimates (the official ones are either non-existent or classified), Poland has lost 0.5–2 billion dollars as a result of this "perestroika." Compared to these numbers, the public debt accumulated during the Gierek rule seems like "pocket money." This unprecedented robbery committed against the Polish nation created a situation in which Poles could own only their labour since their whole capital went to foreign hands. Industrial and bank assets were sold off for about 10 percent of their worth, which made the economy of Poland dependent on other countries. Since economics and politics are almost inseparable, the scale of foreign influence on the Polish economy raised fears of a similar thing happening in the sphere of politics.

Then came about the idea of joining the European Union. Again, no one hesitated, nor did any proper estimates – it was simply "the only way to go."

Historically, the decision to join the EU was made unanimously by the left and the right. Moreover, both sides competed each other on who was to be granted the "honour" of signing the treaty of accession. However, there were no substantive negotiations with the EU. The only talks that occurred concerned merely political and ideological matters of how to subordinate Poland to the EU's bureaucratic structures.

The Poles have never opposed the idea of building common Europe. The thing that raised their doubts, however, has been the ideological foundations of the EU, the dominant role of Germany in its structures, and the place that Poland was to assume within the ranks of this superpower.

Pushing Poland into joining the EU served as a smokescreen for all ongoing economic scandals created by the so called ruling class and the reformers of the early years of Polish independence. As a result, these elites managed to secure their wealth and positions, while their anti-state activities fell into oblivion.

It is interesting that during the time of Poland's accession to the EU both sides of the political spectrum – Law and Justice and Civic Platform on the right, and Democratic Left Alliance on the left – were unanimously in favour of it. This confirms that there are no differences between political left and right in Poland. There is no ideological struggle between them, and the only thing they strive for is power, i.e., the domination over the society. The division between both sides is fictional. It serves as a propaganda that pulls the wool over the society's (as well as the world's) eyes and claims that there is an ideological pluralism in Poland, or that the Polish democracy is in an excellent condition.

Moreover, the ruling class needs this distinction to be able to manipulate society. Usually, elections in Poland are won by the side that is considered less compromised by its ineffectual governance in the preceding years. However, due to the fact that the opposition used to govern in the exact same (bad) way, disoriented citizens either forgot how things were or, simply, have no other options to vote for. The situation resembles a cheap theatre in which the viewers hope that this time they will see an exciting show, but – since the actors are always the same, and only their costumes change – they get fooled and disappointed every time. On the other hand, there are also those who believe that this time it is the libertarians or the nationalists (or yet another minor faction) that will win and bring the necessary change. In reality, however, it does not matter who wins the elections and rules for the next four years.

The form of governance that has crystallised during the last 30 years in Poland is a semi-democratic system in which the dominant position is occupied by the so-called political elites. It has nothing to do with true democratic pluralism. The

system's fundamental principle can be described by the attitude of "we vs. you," with the ruling class (who constitute "the political authority") on the one side, and the society on the other.

All of the substitutes of democracy, like free elections, free media, separation of powers, are merely a façade or propaganda used for covering up financial manipulations, selling off of the country's assets, and seeking scraps that fall from Brussel's table. They are necessary to tame the Poles and the international community. It is a fact that in recent years there has been an infringement of democratic principles in Poland, and there are several indications of that:

First, the balance between particular powers (legislative, executive, judiciary) has been violated for a long time.

Second, free elections are pure fiction – all candidates are determined by the political parties based on their internal lists of accepted individuals.

Three, there are no free media. There are only entities that pose as media, called "official" and "samizdat" publishers. Polish political journalists are fully aware of the problems caused by parties with non-democratic style of leadership, the representatives' dependency on their parties, and the general ineffectiveness of the Sejm. Why are they silent about it? Because it is the only way to guarantee themselves any presence in the world of media dominated by the major parties. It is the same as

during the times of the Polish People's Republic: "We know what we know, but we talk and write only about things we are allowed to do so."

Thousand of members of the bureaucratic force in Poland hamper entrepreneurship, while every new statute generates tremendous costs. Legislation spans for over hundreds of thousands of pages, and there are hundreds of thousands of public officials – in spite of the fact that we cannot afford it. We accumulate debt, issue bonds and pay enormous interests to foreign banks. On the other hand, many elements of the country's infrastructure, like schools *etc.*, are underfunded. Due to the excess and complexity of our laws, we become poorer and more dependent on other countries. We still have not cut off ourselves from the era of the Polish People's Republic. We lack people and politicians who understand the idea of *raison d'état*, who care about the economic development of Poland. It is truly tragic that our political system allows situations in which a person's actions – although destructive for the economy, the country, and the people – may still be perfectly legal. What is worse is that, due to the legality of those actions, many citizens will consider such an individual as completely innocent. Apart from being absurd, this shows how much the consciences of Poles have degenerated over the last three decades.

We should not be surprised that everything is going in the wrong direction, and that sooner or later it will ignite a giant conflict. We do not mean necessarily a civil war, but rather a conflict of an economic, cultural, social, or event religious nature. The actions of our politicians and state's leaders resemble a bad cabaret. In order to see this, one only needs to take a look at newspapers and news channels (naturally, we should always remember not to rely on their opinions and form our own views).

Governance is not a children's game. It is a difficult and complex "job" that requires traits like intellectual input, understanding of how a given political system works, wide imagination and intuition. Moreover, it requires a perfect knowledge of psychological and sociological principles that determine the dynamics of diverse groups, organisations and individuals with differing socio-political views.

In order to develop these qualities, one must possess a great wisdom and a potential to be as humane as it is possible. It is also necessary to be a genuine patriot all the time, not only on special occasions.

Since Polish politicians lack all of the above characteristics, it is not surprising that state of affairs in Poland is as it is – the country is divided, conflicted, and completely confused.

This gives rise to the strong need of a new form of governance, one that would engage ordinary citizens in the decision-making process and end the current elitist, top-down system. Purely "cosmetic" changes (such as "the good change" slogan of the

Law and Justice party) will never do anything to mend the foundations of the Polish political system.

The libertarian and nationalistic groups that have been emerging in recent times are also impotent in this regard. The reason is that they too subscribe to the top-down form of governance and strive for power, while treating society in an instrumental way. These groups seem to lack skills, or maybe even the desire, to create a true alternative, and since they do not go beyond the mainstream slogans, they are quickly sucked into the system.

At some point, a radical change must and will occur. But what for now? Well, the cheap theatre continues its repertoire: giant planes, meetings, celebrations, elections, medals and monuments, anniversaries, scandals, appointments and dismissals, budgets and limousines, shady factions, singing of the national anthem just for show, hypocrisy and contempt for citizens…

And what is the point of all this? The answers are always the same: "For Poland to grow strong and the people to live prosperously" (as Edward Gierek put it), or: "in the name of national interest." Sadly, no politician is able to define it.

The need for change is necessary and justified. Everyone knows it and feels it, however, only few have a real plan of taking a radical step.

1. The Responsibility of Polish Politicians

One of the main reasons behind the existence of the Polish semi-democracy is the fact that our politicians evade the responsibility for the country's affairs and development. Unfortunately, the concept of political responsibility lacks an objective meaning, and thus it is interpreted in numerous ways. Nevertheless, politicians' actions have real political and economic, as well as moral, consequences. In socio-political terms, very often actions that benefit politicians are at the same time harmful to citizens. This stems from the fact that politicians' actions are not guided by Christian ethics, or they simply lack the awareness of being responsible for the fate of the nation that they represent.

This problem becomes especially visible when it comes to amending the Constitution or the introduction of new electoral regulations. People in power know very well that any amendments to the Constitution or electoral laws should benefit society and the state. Instead, they usually shun the responsibility and prepare changes that serve solely their vested interests. While leaving Christian ethics aside, they follow only their party's moral code and, thus, are biased in evaluating their own actions.

Is it then possible to assess actions that are not based on an objective moral responsibility? Moreover, is it necessary for politicians to come up with their own moral codes that often serve as a protection from real responsibility?

Politicians distinguish between objective and subjective morality. Usually, they follow a subjective moral code that suits their current political situation and reflects positions taken on various issues by the major Polish parties (which are generally managed in an authoritarian manner).

It is precisely this cunning that prevents them from amending the Constitution, introducing new electoral laws or elements of direct-democracy that would grant the power to the true sovereign. This stems from the fact that the major parties, as well as interest groups that accompany them, follow their own tribal moral codes. If the political circumstances change, politicians instantly come up with new "moral values" in order to open new ways for their political or material profits. They do not consider this to be immoral or destabilising, they view it simply as beneficial or disadvantageous in a given situation. All beneficiaries of the system automatically adapt to the changing circumstances and thus create a new, stable foundation for their further activity. Political parties follow their own rules, which they call "moral," as long as all of their members agree on them. In reality, however, this "morality" has nothing to do with objective or Christian ethics and responsibility. The major parties define their own systems of values in a way that rarely, or never, corresponds to the country's social and economic reality.

This disparity in understating of ethics by politicians on the one hand and citizens on the other confirms the semi-democratic nature of the Polish political system with its fundamental division of the society into two groups: those in power and those who are governed by them.

That is why it is so important for the people to be able to express their voice, for example, in a nationwide referendum. Decisions made in this way are not subjective but are based on general ethics and social consent.

Naturally, it is the task of the government's agencies to define and execute the rules of systemic harmony between the economic and the socio-political side of a country's life. Only in this way efficient solutions of a political life of a nation can be found. But what kind of agencies do we have in mind, and how should they be elected? Certainly, not in the system of party-determined list of candidates, which compels citizens to run for office in a collective manner. Today, as a result of parties following their subjective moral codes, the representatives are *de facto* elected by those parties' leaders.

According to the objective idea of Christian ethics and democracy, "the representatives of a nation" should be elected by the people. Although it seems plain and simple, it is so only for those who follow their innately held principles of Christian morality.

The quality of people's lives should be assessed on the basis of how a given system is beneficial for them and for the state in general. Citizens, politicians included, should be aware of their joint responsibility for the optimal and moral functioning of the triangle "society – state – economy."

The standard of value for moral behaviour can be based on Christian ethics, which can serve also as a foundation for objective political responsibility. It is time for Poland to overcome the phenomenon of parallel society in which the government follows the aforementioned "we vs. you" principle in its actions toward citizens. First, however, it is necessary to take a closer look at the shape of the political system, which our politicians seem to be incapable of doing. They are so entangled in their political quarrels that they simply lack the time to take a proper care of the economic and social policies of the state.

If that is the situation, then why Polish citizens, i.e., the sovereign, cannot take matters in their own hands and start making decisions on issues that concern them directly?

The answer is simple: despite the fact that according to Article 4 of the Constitution of Poland, the power is exercised **by the Nation directly or through their representatives,**[43] the direct form of governance has been completely abandoned in the Polish decision-making process. Therefore, the people can only rely on their representatives, namely, the government and the parliament, with the Sejm in the forefront.

In Poland, the Sejm is the main decision-making agency. It is supposed to be composed of the country's elite, i.e., the best and the most independent individuals, capable of understanding the most important problems, and acting on the social teachings of the Church and the Nation's interest.

Let us then take a look at the current reality of the Sejm.

Our representatives do not feel responsible for the country's fate because, above all, they represent the interests of their parties. They do not work for the good of the country, but rather adapt their actions to the will of their party's leaders.

Why? Because they depend on them; it is the leaders who put them in the position of power, not genuine electoral laws.

The methods of "appointing" the representatives are the same in all parties and electoral committees. The leader appoints candidates who later become "the

---

[43]   All citations from the Constitution of Poland are from an official translation available at: https://www.sejm.gov.pl/prawo/konst/angielski/kon1.htm (translator's note).

representatives of the Nation," given that the party crosses the electoral threshold.

That is how the governing elite is chosen in Poland. And it governs in the same way it is chosen: irresponsibly, with the party's interest as an end, short-sightedly, based on personal sympathies and antipathies. Instead of making decisions based on national interest, the Sejm occupies itself with issues such as Smolensk crash, shady past of parties' members, inspection of their personal files, and shaming opponents or promoting bootlickers.

The Nation's "chosen ones" also lack the sense of guilt for socio-economic crises, which is an another example of them evading the responsibility. They focus only on party quarrels and obedience to their leaders, while seeking the opportunities to maximise their own gains (in terms of money and re-election). All of this leads the country into unnecessary conflict and gradual demise.

As a result of this way of governance, millions of Poles have emigrated abroad, families became divided, many absurd laws have been enacted, the country's assets are sold off, making it poorer. Do the people in power feel responsible for this situation? Do they feel ashamed of their egoistic actions? Has any of the cabinets of the last 30 years apologised for its errors? Sadly, these are only rhetorical questions. The only answer we hear is: "It is not our fault, it is theirs."

2. Democracy, But What Kind of Democracy?

Democracy, as some people believe, is not superior to other political systems, nor is it eternal or immune to any destabilising factors. The evidence for that lies in the fact that there are several fundamental forms of democratic governance. Therefore, it is difficult to define which of them is the most functional and effective. According to many political scientists, the best one is the Swiss direct democracy. However, it also has disadvantages. Moreover, the political or economic success of a given country does not always correspond to the level of functionality or dysfunctionality of its form of governance.

Nevertheless, everyone agrees that the most effective form of democracy is the one that brings the process of governance as closely to the people as it is possible and engages them in decision-making both on the local and the national level.

There is no perfect democracy – all of its forms require constant corrections and adjustments. As a system, it is characterised by uncertainty; it has to constantly face the challenges of the postmodern world. Certainly, it is not "the best of all political systems."

Suffice it to say that the presidential system of the United States, semi-presidential one in France, as well as the German system, or even the Swiss one, leave a lot to be desired.

It is crucial to implement the principles of a given form of democracy in a proper and efficient manner, which is often indirectly determined by a country's historical experience, geopolitical situation, and the level of development.

The level of active participation of citizens in the political process on the one hand, and the operational efficiency of the state – including its local agencies – on the other, are certainly the two most important criteria for assessing the functionality (or dysfunctionality) of a given form of democracy.

Since democracy and conflicts, as phenomena, are closely connected, every democratic system should provide instruments that would contribute to their resolution. Such tools are worked out within the frameworks of a broadly defined political culture. What is a political culture? It is inextricably linked with the development of civil society, which is further determined by the functionality of a given democracy.

The concept of civil society, in its optimal meaning, refers to the activities in the social, economic, and political spheres, which constitute the elements of the political decision-making process. In this context, a political culture is the sum total of attitudes, values, and patterns of behaviour that

determine all interactions between those in power and the rest of citizens.

When it comes to Poland, the values I am referring to are derived from Christian ethics and the Polish political traditions. The functioning of the triangle "society – state – economy" in the Polish democratic system should be based on the Constitution which is the fundamental and supreme law.

The current Constitution of Poland was adopted in 1997 at the end of the term of social democratic faction. Socialists found the moment very convenient since the president of Poland was at the time Aleksander Kwaśniewski, a post-communist and a leader of the Democratic Left Alliance, who assumed the office in December of 1995.

In the constitutional referendum, citizens were asked only about the bill that was accepted by the then left-wing parliamentary majority. Voter turnout was only 43 percent, of which 53 percent voted in favour. It means that only 6.4 millions of citizens eligible to vote took part in the referendum. Thus, it cannot be assumed that the current Constitution reflects the political views of the majority of Poles. Unfortunately, when it comes to the quality of the Constitution of Poland, an average cookbook is written in a more logical and intelligible fashion.

From the very beginning, the Constitution was impotent in regard to numerous difficulties that the country had been struggling with. It introduced many legal and legislative ambiguities. It does not regulate the problem of Poland's political dependency during the communist era, the apparatus of coercion of the previous system, or the collaboration of many state agencies with the USSR. It lacks any reference to the problem of Polish expatriates, expropriations, stripping of citizenship, and many others.

The Constitution invokes the system of "direct democracy," but in reality the whole governance is carried out top-down, and all "democratic" decisions are made by the undemocratic Sejm or by cabinets whose members follow their parties' leaders.

It is interesting that we do not know the actual authors of the document…

Apart from being designed in a very wily way, it is also hedged around by so many laws that people in power can interpret it as they like – and they do so since they are incapable of taking a real responsibility for the country.

The history of our country shows that while designing a constitution we should consider the spirit of the times. If we want our Constitution to be up to the modern standards, it needs some serious amendments. It should provide legal instruments that would allow us to carry out our own, sovereign policies, keep the country safe, and to directly influence the nation's fate.

It is important that we define citizens' participation in the country's decision-making process in terms of specific laws. By doing this we can propose certain amendments that would introduce a proper form of referendum – a binding tool of expressing citizens' will and social supervision – and popular initiative that would allow us to initiate a referendum whenever we deem it necessary. In short, in order to open the possibility for citizens to actively participate in shaping the country's future, we need a new constitution.

The way in which our current political elites consolidate their power – by exploiting their dominant position – is at odds with true moral principles. As it was already mentioned, politicians invent their own codes of ethics and conduct. However, crookedness, financial chicanery, constant lying, and corruption cannot provide a foundation of any ethics. Grassroots democracy is the only way to fill our political life with integrity and conduct anchored in Christian and humane ethics. The new constitution should fully protect citizens' rights to decide on matters that concern them directly.

3. Why Direct Democracy?

Introducing certain elements of grassroots democracy in our country seems like a rather simple task. Let us take a look at some ways of doing it. As a starting point of our analysis, we have to assume Article 4 of the Constitution of Poland:

1. Supreme power in the Republic of Poland shall be vested in the Nation.
2. The Nation shall exercise such power **directly** or through their representatives.

The word "directly" is of crucial importance here, for it establishes the principle of grassroots form of governance, i.e., by citizens for citizens.

The most important element of direct democracy – the system in which citizens participate in the decision-making – is a nationwide referendum that is legally binding and does not require a validity threshold. As such, it is an instrument of social control over the government; its serves as a tool for shaping the political system and expressing society's will.

Although the Constitution of 1997 mentions a referendum, it is not society who is eligible to initiate it, but the Sejm or the president with the Senate's approval. Such referendum has nothing to do with genuine grassroots democracy or the will of Polish citizens (the actual sovereign).

Fig. 1. The basic instruments of direct democracy.

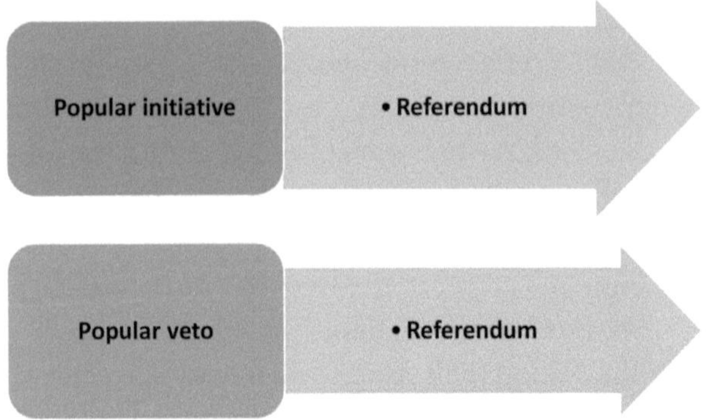

Source: own work.

Since only the people understand their problems directly, it is them who have to initiate the necessary changes. Such grassroots action should be followed by a nationwide referendum that leads to an amendment of a given law or the Constitution. When it comes to the revision of particular legal acts, the proper instrument for that – as it is in the Swiss system – should be popular veto, which constitutes a tool for protesting against an existing statute or proposing a new one (see Fig. 1).

In Switzerland, popular veto can be initiated at the request of 50,000 citizens. In Poland, the number of required signatures could be, for instance, 250,000. Apart from that, there should be set a period of, let us say, 180 days for collecting signatures. Veto should be followed by a referendum with a "yes or no" type of question, **without any validity threshold**. Why should there be no validity threshold? Because it would constitute an additional obstacle, and such obstacles are contradictory to democracy. Those who do not participate in referendum, vote passively – by accepting its results.

Similarly, popular initiative should also result in an amendment of an existing regulation or introduction of a new provision into the Constitution (see Fig. 1). This instrument would also be a tool for initiating a referendum with a "yes or no" type of question. In Switzerland, popular initiative requires 100,000 signatures in order to be initiated. In Poland, it could be, for instance, 500,000, and the optimal period for collecting signatures could be 18 months.

It should be pointed out that referendum is the most important instrument of direct democracy, through which it is society who decides on the state's matters. In order for it be held, it has to be initiated directly by those who demand certain changes in their legal system.

Popular veto (which concerns the normal legislative level) and popular initiative (which concerns

the Constitutional level) are procedural instruments of direct democracy that should always result in binding legal changes, and they should be free of any validity thresholds.

After the people's vote, the government, as the executive agency, should be obliged to introduce accepted changes within, let us say, one year.

Implementing those instruments in Poland would bring a shift of power from the political parties and the state agencies to the hands of the people, bringing us closer to the ideal of a true civil society (see Fig. 2).

Fig. 2. The power shift in the Polish political process.

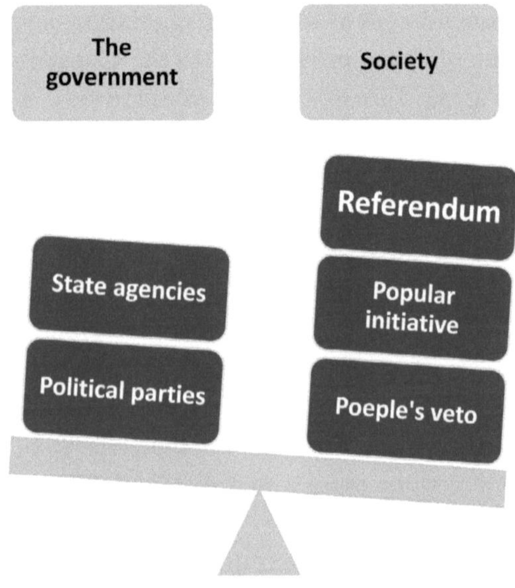

Source: own work.

In the next chapters we shall discuss in detail the three basic instruments of grassroots democracy, which – in our opinion – should become the unquestionable foundation of a healthy and democratic political system in Poland.

4. Referendum

In the future, referendum should become a democratic form of social supervision over the officialdom, a tool for shaping the political system, and a binding expression of the society's will.

It is a paradox that although the Constitution of Poland makes referendum possible, the relevant provisions – as well as the whole document, actually – is practically useless. They are chaotic, inconsequential, and impractical.

The Constitution distinguishes three kinds of a nation-wide referendum:

- as a way of granting of consent for ratification of an international agreement, by virtue of which the Republic of Poland delegates to an international organisation or international institution the competence of organ of State authority in relation to certain matters (Article 90);
- in matters of particular importance to the State (Article 125);
- in matters of amending the Constitution (Article 235).

The first and the third kind are specific in the sense that they concern an existing statute or an international agreement which citizens are to accept or reject.

The concept of "matters of particular importance to the State" (Article 125), however, is ambiguous. A referendum of this sort concerns only general issues and cannot be considered as superior to any state agencies' decisions; it only specifies what kind of solutions the agencies can undertake in the future. As a result, such referendum does not concern matters that have already been regulated. In other words, there is no way of amending any statute through referendum – the law is "sacred" and cannot be repealed, regardless of how absurd or outdated it may be.

Moreover, according to the Constitution, referendum is always optional. Naturally, it is citizens who decide whether it will be held – everything depends on politicians' goodwill.

Let us take a closer look at Article 125 of the current Constitution of Poland. It contains a specific provision concerning a nationwide referendum, which in its current form constitutes merely a substitute a of grassroots democracy. The Article provides for holding a referendum in matters of utmost importance to the Polish state. Supposedly, it is based on Article 4 which states that the supreme power in the Republic of Poland shall be exercised by the Nation directly or through their representatives. "Directly" should mean in a grassroots manner, with an active participation of citizens, i.e., the unquestionable sovereign.

REFERENDUM
Article 125

1. A nationwide referendum may be held in respect of matters of particular importance to the State.
2. The right to order a nationwide referendum shall be vested in the Sejm, to be taken by an absolute majority of votes in the presence of at least half of the statutory number of Deputies, or in the President of the Republic with the consent of the Senate given by and absolute majority vote taken in the presence of at least half of the statutory number of Senators.
3. A result of a nationwide referendum shall be binding, if more that half of the number of those having the right to vote have participated in it.
4. The validity of a nationwide referendum and the referendum referred to in Article 235, para. 6, shall be determined by the Supreme Court.
5. The principles of and procedures for the holding of a referendum shall be specified by statute.

The above provision has nothing to do with grassroots democracy. Why?

First, no one is able to specify what the concept of "matters of utmost importance to the State" means in concrete terms. There are many different suggestions of what it means: the introduction of the common European currency, the closing of the Ukrainian border, fighting corruption *etc.*

Second, a nationwide referendum may be initiated only by the Sejm or the President with the consent of the Senate. Additionally, it requires an absolute majority of votes taken in the presence of at least half of the statutory members of a given body. This poses a virtually impenetrable barrier that makes any referendum inaccessible for citizens. Society can only stand aside and watch its political elite at work.

Third, a referendum is binding only if a half of the eligible to vote participate, which is completely at odds with any democratic norms. By setting such a validity threshold, the government limits the possibilities of making democratic decisions in the country by abandoning the rule that passive voting (i.e., not participating) should also be considered valid.

In order to effectively engage the sovereign in the political process, Articles 90, 125, and 235 (see Annex IV) of the Constitution should be amended. Their current wording is incompatible with the idea

of direct democracy, and they do not vest the power in citizens.

It should be emphasised that the Polish Constitution does not provide for an obligatory referendum, which is a grave error. It is specifically the case of the Articles regarding issues of international agreements (Article 90) and amendments to the Constitution (Article 235). Since they do not make a referendum mandatory in these matters, they should be changed and supplemented with a provision compelling the government to hold a referendum not only on the most urgent issues but also on those that are not specified by the Constitution (Article 125).

Apart from that, there should be a new article concerning a referendum that would allow society to express its will through popular initiative in matters of amending the Constitution or statutes (through popular veto) – we will discuss it later.

New provisions introducing an obligatory referendum and replacing the current Articles 90, 125, and 235, could read as follows:

OBLIGATORY REFERENDUM
1. A national referendum shall concern:
   a) amending the Constitution of the Republic o Poland;
   b) accession to collective security organisations or supranational communities;

    c) matters considered the most urgent, which are not specified in the Constitution and whose time-span exceeds one year.

2. A national referendum shall also concern:

    a) popular initiatives concerning a complete amendment of the Constitution of the Republic of Poland;

    b) popular initiatives concerning a partial amendment of the Constitution of the Republic of Poland presented in a form of specific provisions;

    c) popular veto in matters of repealing or amending an existing statute.

3. The Supreme Court shall adjudicate upon the validity of an obligatory referendum.

4. The Council of Ministers shall implement the decisions made through an obligatory referendum within one year.

(© M. Matyja, Public Domain)

These provisions contain two fundamental sections. The first one **compels the government** to hold a referendum every time it wants to make amendments to the Constitution or to access a collective security organisation or supranational community (see Fig. 3).

Fig. 3. A referendum ordered by the government according to the proposed provisions.

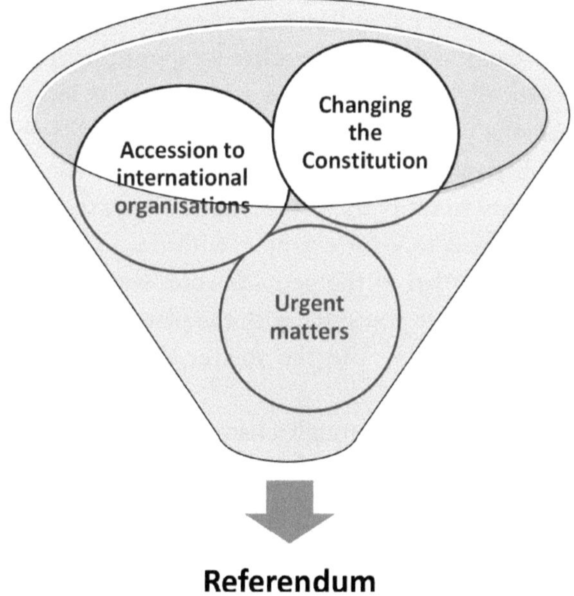

Source: Own work.

The section 1.c. requires a more detailed explanation. It replaces the ambiguous provision in Article 125 of the current Constitution concerning "the matters of utmost important for the State."

A new provision should state: "matters considered the most urgent, which are not specified in the Constitution of the Republic of Poland, whose timespan exceeds one year." It is best to illustrate it with an example: Suppose that the Polish government intends to purchase weapons abroad, which is an enormous task requiring serious expenditures (covered naturally with taxpayers money). The Constitution does not regulate weapons purchases specifically, the contract of purchase lasts longer than one year, and the weapons are supposed to be supplied over several years. The government has the authority to ratify the contract, however, after that it is obliged to – for example, within a year – put the whole plan to the people's vote. The question should be: "Do you agree with the plan of purchasing weapons…?" And the answer should be only "yes" or "no."

In this way – through a nationwide referendum with no validity threshold – the sovereign makes the ultimate, binding decision regarding the purchase of weapons. Other similar examples may include: construction of gas pipes, purchase of trains, deportation of foreign criminals *etc.*

It is understandable that the expression "matters considered the most urgent, which are not specified by the Constitution, whose timespan exceeds one year" – although better than the original one – is still not perfect. It leaves the Sejm a room for interpretations, since the very idea of "urgent matters" may also be debatable. In order to avoid that, the concept should be specified by statute. It cannot be done in the Constitution itself due to obvious, formal reasons.

When it comes to Article 90 (see Annex IV), it suggests clearly that a referendum, as an instrument of expressing the people's consent regarding an international agreement, is only optional. The situation is identical in the case of amending the Constitution (Article 235). A nationwide referendum is considered as an exceptional procedure, initiated solely by the Sejm and the Senate. Due to this fact, both Articles have nothing to do with grassroots democracy and everything to do with the "goodwill" of the people in power. That is why it is necessary to introduce an obligatory referendum into the Polish political system.

The section 2 of the proposed provisions refers to the people's participation in the legislative process (see Fig. 4). It would be a completely new element in the Polish political system. By assuming the role of the initiators, citizens would be able to influence it through initiative or veto. As it has already been mentioned, the difference is that the former aims at amending the Constitution, while the latter amends statutes. Nevertheless, both instruments function through the process of nationwide referendum.

Fig. 4. A referendum ordered by the citizens according to the proposed provisions.

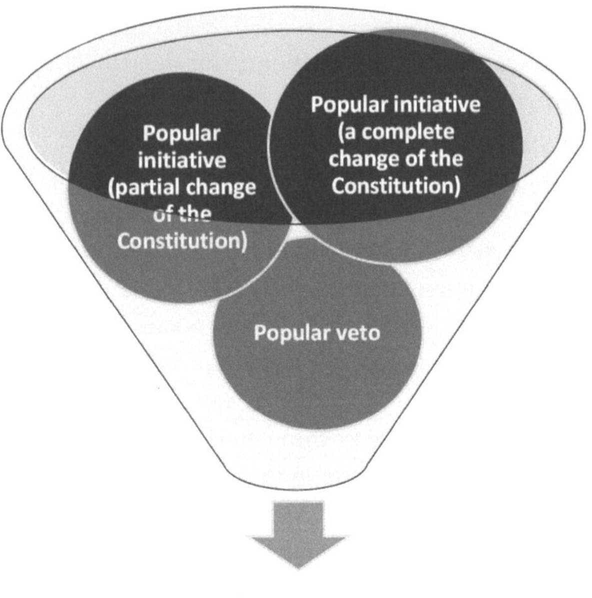

Source: Own work.

The proposed amendments to the Constitution of Poland are intended to provoke thought and need further refinement. They should be seen as an incentive to make changes necessary to introduce the instruments of referendum in the Polish political system.

It should be added that it would not be necessary for a citizen to go to the polling station every time there was a referendum. In Switzerland, 90 percent of the eligible to vote do so by mail. Any information regarding a referendum, along with voting forms with "yes or no" question, are sent to citizens' homes. Since taking part in a referendum is dictated by the sense of civic duty, validity thresholds are pointless and at odds with common sense.

Switzerland is about to introduce the system of electronic voting. It is worth mentioning that a similar system is being implemented in Sobótka commune (Wrocław county) where a project of grassroots democracy has been initiated by Mr. Janusz Zagórski. This shows that direct democracy is not a complete novelty to Poland after all.

5. Popular initiative

Popular initiative is a political tool that grants citizens and various social groups the right to initiate amendments to the Constitution, i.e., to create new laws. The scope of its application differs among countries. In Switzerland, it can be used to make partial or complete amendments to the constitution. It also requires 100,000 signatures collected within 18 months in order to be valid. The Swiss may demand to make amendments, to repeal existing constitutional provisions, or to introduce new regulations. Such initiative may concern both specific and general matters. Any initiative that ends with a successful collection of signatures automatically results in a nationwide referendum. In 1999, Poland has passed the citizens' legislative initiative act. However, it contains a number of provisions that substantially limit the possibility of its practical use as an efficient instrument of grassroots influence on the Polish legislation by citizens.

The Polish version of popular initiative – unlike the Swiss one – enables changes only on the statutory level, and in no way can it affect the Constitution. Legislative initiative is the right to propose a bill, which allows citizens to present a new legal solution concerning issues not regulated by statutes or to amend an existing legal act. In this regard it is similar to the Swiss system. It is interesting, however, that according to the Constitution of Poland, there are **only several specified** entities that have the right of legislative initiative:

- The President;
- The Council of Ministers;
- The Deputies (a group of 15 or a parliamentary committee);
- The Senate (as a whole).

Polish citizens have gained the right of legislative initiative in 1999. In order to be exercises properly, it requires establishing a committee that collects 100,000 signatures within 3 months (Article 118 of the Polish Constitution). Any bill proposed in this manner has to be accompanied by a report documenting its financial consequences.

The provision reads as follows:

Article 118

1. The right to introduce legislation shall belong to Deputies, to the Senate, to the President of the Republic and to the Council of Ministers.
2. The right to introduce legislation shall also belong to a group of at least

100,000 citizens having the right to vote in elections to the Sejm. The procedure in such matter shall be specified by statute.

3. Sponsors, when introducing a bill to the Sejm, shall indicate the financial consequences of its implementation.

In the next stage, the bill is passed to the Marshall of the Sejm, and after that the process is identical as in the case of any other legislative act. Due to the complicated procedure, as well as short signature collection period, the number of bills proposed by citizens that are actually discussed in the Sejm is very low. **Apart from that, in Switzerland, similar initiative would have to be put to the vote in a referendum, whereas in Poland grassroots democracy ends already at the signature collection stage.** At the beginning of the legislative process, the bill is termed as "parliamentary printed matter" and is given a specific number (see Fig. 5). From this point, deputies begin discussing the proposed legislation, while citizens lose control over its shape and become passive observers. Thus, in Poland, the initiative is essentially nothing more than a citizens' petition to the politicians in power.

From the logical point of view, any legislative initiative should be put to the vote in a nation-wide referendum, as it is in Switzerland. Only then

a given political system can be considered as giving its citizens a real and creative possibility to participate in the political decision-making.

It is also noteworthy that the initiative is further limited by the fact that some projects can be proposed only by a specific entity. The best illustration is the State Budget Act which can be proposed only by the Council of Ministers (Article 221 of the Constitution of Poland). Another example is a bill on the amendment to the Constitution: the initiative belongs to a group of at least 1/5 of the statutory number of Deputies, to the Senate, or to the President (Article 235, sec. 1). This means that Polish citizens lack even a theoretical possibility of a grassroots way of amending the Constitution.

Fig. 5. Legislative initiative according to the current Constitution.

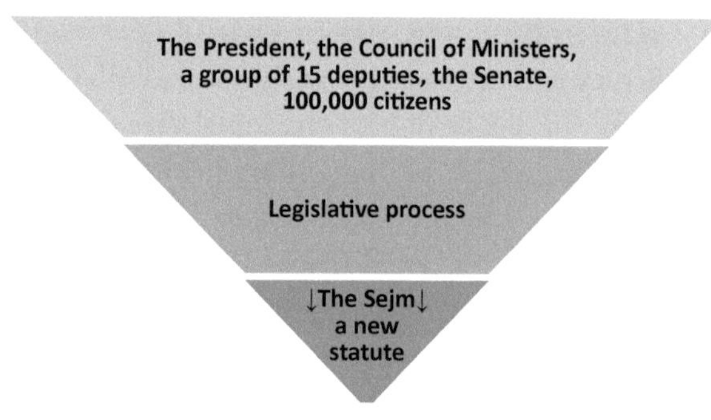

Source: Own work.

As an element of grassroots democracy, citizens' initiative should be a tool of creativity

and innovation. It should be initiated by citizens themselves and lead to a binding referendum in which they would make their final decision without having to comply with any validity thresholds.

The goal of an initiative should be to introduce new laws by amending or adding provisions to the Constitution. This means that it cannot function only on the statutory level, and it should always result in modifying the Constitution itself.

The number of signatures required and the time for their collection also needs to be revised. If we compare Poland to Switzerland, it seems that 500,000 signatures with 18 month collection period would be a realistic option. It would be enough to organise rallies and campaigns in various social and political circles.

Fig. 6. Popular initiative according to the proposed constitutional amendments.

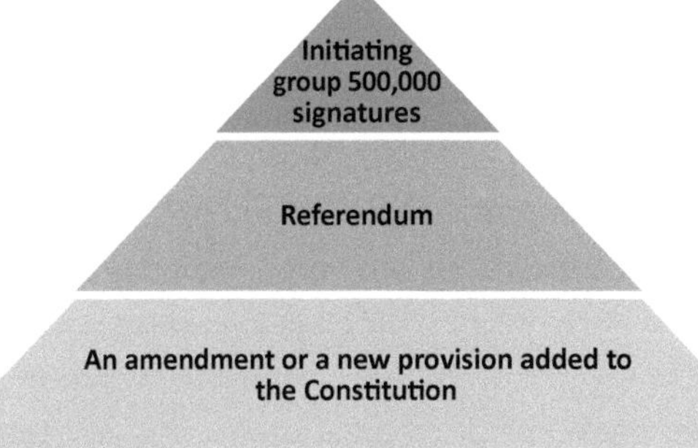

Source: Own work.

A new article introducing a proper instrument of popular initiative should read as follows:

Popular initiative
(© M. Matyja, Public Domain)

1. All citizens of the Republic of Poland, as well as socio-political groupings, shall retain the right to exercise popular initiative.

2. Popular initiative is valid if a registered initiating committee collects at least 500,000 signatures of citizens eligible to vote and presents its project to the Council of Ministers within 18 months.

3. The Council of Ministers adjudicates on the constitutionality of a project proposed through popular initiative and its conformity to the international law binding upon the Republic of Poland.

4. A project proposed through popular initiative shall be put to the vote in a nationwide referendum.

Let us note that the proposed provisions do not mention the Sejm, but only the Council of Ministers. Since the government is the executive power, it is its duty to assure that the procedure is completed efficiently and leads to a nationwide referendum (see Fig. 6). Another government's task is to check whether a given initiative complies to the international law that Poland has obliged to obey by signing certain treaties and agreements.

Let us take a closer look at how it could work in practice:

Article 168 of the Constitution of Poland concerns taxes and charges set by units of local government:

Article 168

To the extent established by statute, units of local government shall have the right to set the level of local taxes and charges.

Local government strives to be independent in terms of its budget and financial policies. The current constitutional provision, however, limits this independence and cedes the regulation of this matter to a statute, making it, paradoxically, superior to the Constitution (there are other such cases).

It is therefore necessary to amend Article 168. In order to do that, an initiating committee needs to be established, whose goal would be to collect 500,000 signatures within 18 months. The initiators would be obliged to present a new wording of the article, which could read as follows:

Article 168

Units of local government shall have the right to set the level of local taxes and charges by themselves.

Collecting half a million signatures within a year and a half is not an easy task, but given the dissatisfaction of the communes with the financial policies imposed on them, it is not impossible. It would be necessary to organise an informative campaign, which is an element of any democracy, not only its grassroots form.

When the signatures are collected, the project is proposed to the government whose duty is to set the date of a nationwide referendum. This process is free from any interference on the part of the Sejm or the Senate.

Citizens make a decision by answering a question whether they want to change Article 168 and, thus, to introduce a new financial policy and tax system on the local level. The decision is binding and final. The Council of Ministers, as an executive body, has one year to amend the Constitution.

In case the citizens answer "no," nothing changes, although – only seemingly. For the referendum send a signal that there is a problem with the tax policy on the local level. Now, the Parliament and the government have to take into consideration that many citizens are opposed to the current regulations in this field. But what would happen if those bodies remained indifferent to the matter? Well, they would be compelled to do something anyway due to the very possibility of another initiative, which – this time – may result in a "yes" vote.

This is the essence of grassroots democracy. It simply does not stop. Naturally, there could be other initiatives, which would not necessarily aim at amending any constitutional provision, but rather at introducing a completely new one. For instance, a provision concerning punishments for individuals guilty of economic scandals, a ban on the privatisation of industrial plants, a ban on selling Polish financial institutions to foreigners, a percentage of foreigners allowed to reside in Poland, or a change of electoral laws from undemocratic to democratic ones *etc.* One could provide many similar examples.

Anyway, the people in power should rest reassured. Although citizens may propose any projects they want, collecting half a million signatures is difficult, and even then the way to "win" a referendum is long. Moreover, collecting signatures requires time, energy, and money, which means that usually referenda will be held only in the most important matters.

6. Popular veto

Popular veto, known mostly in Switzerland, is a method of social control over the laws made by politicians. It is a form of protest that makes it impossible for the people in power to create laws which would benefit only them, instead of the society as a whole. In Switzerland, where popular veto has functioned well for the last 150 years, the disputes among the major parties are completely different from those in Poland. They exercise their power by delegating representatives to the seven-member Federal Council, which constitutes the Swiss executive branch. Due to that, the parties are compelled to seek a consensus on all important matters they deal with.

Moreover, all political factions that comprise the Swiss parliament are aware that if they enact a law against the wishes of their voters, sooner or later it will be repealed through popular veto. Due to this, the parliament does not pursue projects that would prompt a general opposition from citizens.

Essentially, popular veto is a method of raising an objection against solutions existing in a current political system. Instead of taking a matter to the

The Polish Sejm is a caricature of democracy and one of the main reasons for the disfunction of the Polish political system. It mocks society by making citizens elect unwanted candidates determined by parties' leaders. In this way, any remains of the true democratic elements in our system are undermined, and the politically dependent media not only applaud this infringement but also support the actions of the Sejm elected through a *de facto* illegitimate electoral system.

Confused by the media and politicians, the Poles vote without even realising that regardless of whom they elect, it will not change anything in the state's socio-economic policies that have been continued for years now. So far, none of the parties has presented any complex plan for socio-economic reforms or for improving the political system.

streets, this instrument allows citizens to veto any law they disagree with.

In Poland, the situation is different. Political parties are doing everything to gain as much power as they can. They rule with a disregard for their political rivals, as well as citizens in general, and act on their particular, oligarchical interests, while pushing the people out of the decision-making process. The law they make is instrumental to their goals, and the only way for Poles to oppose this is to take it to the streets. The sad truth, however, is that no matter how loud the protests are, they are doomed to fail. The people of Poland should have the possibility to object to laws made by politicians by putting them to the vote *via* popular veto.

Similarly to other countries with indirect or parliamentary democracy, such instrument does not exist in Poland. With the dominant position of political parties, popular veto would be an innovative and efficient tool to counter their influence.

If we look at the population of Switzerland, popular veto in Poland should be organised by the order of, approximately, 250,000 citizens eligible to vote. Such a number would be enough to put to the vote an existing statute or to propose a new one.

The results (for or against) would be binding. Theoretically, it seems very simple, and the most interesting thing about it is that the procedure itself is also quite easy in practice.

Let us, for a moment, take a look at this issue from another point of view. Although popular veto does not have to be used everyday, the people in power do have to face its "threat" daily. This alone would make voting in the parliament more cautious, for politicians and their parties would have to consider the opinions of various social groups or society as a whole.

A provision introducing popular veto into the Polish Constitution would certainly be an innovative move, and it would equip citizens with real possibility to control and make laws. Instead of complaining, they would be able to take the initiative into their own hands and, by collecting the necessary number of signatures, change any harmful regulations. It should be emphasised that the decision whether to accept or reject a statute would have to be made by the majority of the participants, and that the Polish government would be obliged to act on it.

Again, the Polish political elites should not worry in excess – collecting 250,000 signatures is not easy and requires a lot of time and organisation. The most important factor here is politicians' awareness of the fact that there exists such a tool of social control over the government, and that it can be easily used against them. This would compel any ruling party to actually consider the opinions of their voters and their trust in them. Figure 7 illustrates the proposed procedure of popular veto in Poland.

Fig. 7. The proposed procedure of popular veto in Poland.

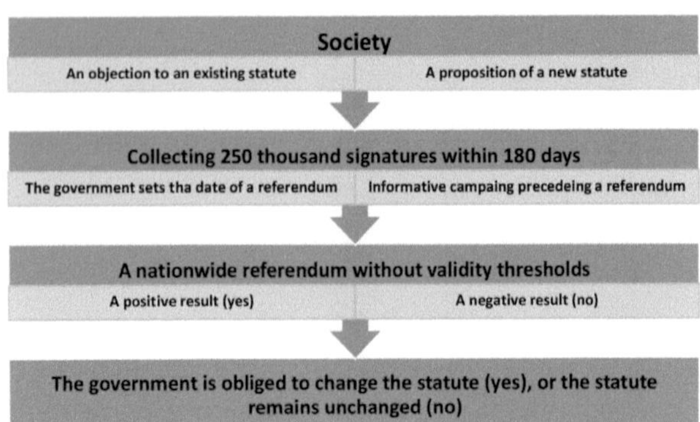

Source: Own work.

A proper constitutional provision introducing popular veto into the Polish political system should be analogical to the one regarding popular initiative and could read as follows:

Popular veto

(© M. Matyja, Public Domain)

1. All citizens of the Republic of Poland, as well as socio-political groupings, shall retain the right to exercise popular veto.
2. Popular veto is valid if a registered vetoing committee collects at least 250,000 signatures of citizens eligible to vote and presents its project to the Council of Ministers within 18 months.

3. The Council of Ministers adjudicates on the constitutionality of a project proposed through popular veto and its conformity to the international law binding upon the Republic of Poland.
4. A project proposed through popular veto shall be put to a vote in a nationwide referendum.

Let us assume that popular veto already exists in the Polish political system. This means that there is a provision, based on Article 4, stating that at the order of 250,000 citizens a referendum is held in order to amend or introduce a new statute.

Now, let us imagine the following example: we know that every newly-elected party makes changes to the laws of education system, which results in organisational chaos and angers students, parents, and teachers.

Therefore, the best solution is to object to the current statute – whose only proponent was the Minister of Education – and to propose a new one. But who can do this? Well, anybody; every citizen eligible to vote may propose a popular veto. Naturally, it is easier to collect the required signatures and to get a positive final result if the initiative is put forward by some political or social organisation. Let us assume that the Polish Teachers' Union, with a vast support of parents representing diverse circles (working class, intellectual, rich and poor, rural and urban), proposes a project of a veto.

People are fed up with educational experiments carried out on their children. Due to the existence of popular veto, they do not have to write complaints (which are ignored, anyway) and appeal to politicians – they just have to collect the signatures within the established time limit.

The vetoing committee presents the Council of Ministers its project, for instance – a following question: **"Are you in favour of changing the Education System Act and reinstating the previous model of educational system?"**

Anyone who knows the reality of Polish schools – namely, teachers and parents (not to mention students) – will answer "yes." The referendum is preceded by an informative campaign where different views are presented and promoted. Naturally, some political parties will exploit the whole matter to boost their ratings.

The government has the right to defend its newly introduced changes, and thus it will call to vote "no." On the other hand, the majority of citizens will probably be of different opinion. Everybody has the right to their own views and to promote them. Any attempts at making the referendum a purely ideological event will fail because the problem it concerns is very narrow and specific. Parents, driven solely by the idea of ensuring the best education and development opportunities for their children, ignore fairy tales propagated by political parties.

Everyone who considers the issue important will take part in voting, as it would be the right thing to do. Naturally, there is no validity threshold, and the results are binding. If the majority answers "no," everything stays the same. However, if the majority votes "yes," then the government has one year to repeal the new statute and reinstate the previous one.

It all seems simple. The ultimate decision belongs to the sovereign, so – regardless of the outcome – citizens have only themselves to blame.

We should, however, ask ourselves whether any Minister would dare to propose changes to the Education System Act in the first place? In the system of grassroots democracy they would probably think twice before doing it – due to the possibility of reversing their decision through a referendum. Maybe they would fear losing their jobs or actually learn to respect the people and never come up with similar ideas in the future?

Let us now come back to reality. The semi-democracy in Poland is a system of top-down governance without any possibility citizens influencing in directly. As a result, government officials act as kings without a crown, who usurp the right to decide on what is good and bad for the country and its people.

On what basis a governmental official, even as high as a Minister, decides on the fortune or misfortune of Polish students? Does a soulless, incompetent bureaucratic machine have a right to determine the fate of Polish families?

Although popular veto is mainly an instrument of defence against harmful attitudes and actions of politicians, such as those exemplified by the problem of our educational system, in fact it can be used to oppose any law.

7. Power Shift in the Polish Political System

Our *complementary model of democracy for Poland* anticipates a long-awaited power shift in the political process. Its implementation would yield an array of positive results that not only would be beneficial to citizens but also would allow them to assume the proper role of the country's sovereign (see Fig. 8). Other improvements include:

First, the decrease of the Sejm's powerful position. Voters would become a natural opposition to political parties who would be compelled to consider people's opinions.

Although society would gain its rightful place in the decision-making process, it would not be the most important thing. The people would be finally able to efficiently supervise the parliament's and the government's activity. Thus, the Sejm and the Senate would have to stop acting as a king without a crown. They would be aware that any law they propose could be opposed by citizens and put to the vote through popular veto. Due to this, the government would also become much more modest in its decisions. Society would become the supervisor of all state agencies.

Many critics of direct democracy consider weakening the position of the parliament as a disadvantage. **Paradoxically, however, if we take a closer look at the current state of the Polish political system, it will become obvious that the country needs to break the omnipotence of its parliament.** The deputies should represent the interests of their voters and consult with them, and the people should be able to defend themselves through veto or initiative. The parliament has to become more civil and democratic.

Second, demonstrations, marches, and protests would no longer be the only way for society to express its dissatisfaction with politics. Popular initiative and veto are the most efficient forms of a legal and peaceful protest. By becoming more aware of those instruments, society becomes more civil and takes greater responsibility for the country.

Third, apart from the parliament, political parties' also lose significance in direct democracy. Citizens would no longer have to rely on them, for the people themselves could make vital decisions. Party membership would lose its appeal since there would be other possibilities to influence the state's policies. Due to the effectiveness of popular veto, initiative, and referendum the role of major parties with non-democratic leadership would be significantly diminished. In short, their political monopoly – as well as their dominance over the nation – would be broken, while at the same time society would regain a genuine influence on the country's politics.

Fourth, in a system of direct democracy, the government functions only as an executive body. Its tasks include efficient organisation of referenda and implementation of their results (amending statutes or the Constitution).

Fifth, state bureaucracy would no longer be uncontrollable and omnipotent (currently no one is able to comprehend its decisions, regulations *etc.*). Society should use popular veto to reduce the overgrown numbers of public officials. Since it is the people who pay taxes and take part in making political decisions, they should have the right to demand a proper treatment in public offices.

Fig 8. A new political structure in complementary democracy.

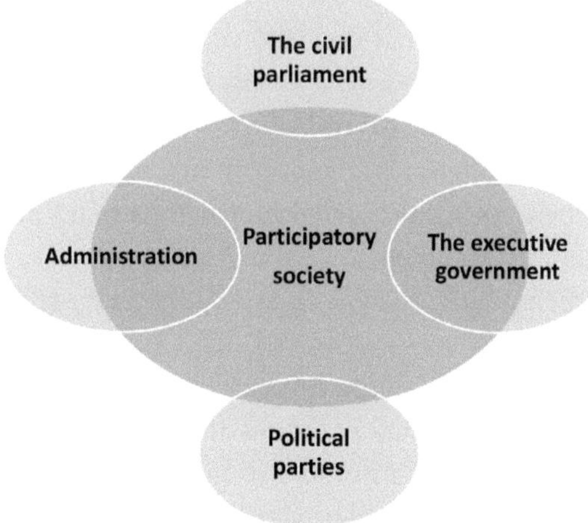

Source: Own work.

Sixth, the awareness of being a part of the political process would cause a burst of positive energy among society. As a result, the people would start to feel co-responsible for the present and the future of the country. On the other hand, those who have been rather passive up to this point would gain a sense of being appreciated and needed, which would reignite their interest in politics. The ultimate effect would be an evolution of the Polish political culture and the formation of a fully civil, participatory society. The process of political socialisation would finally be put back on a proper track. Debates preceding referenda would become more substantive and less ideological. The reason is that the people – who know best what they need – would vote for their own good; they would not have to follow the party line anymore.

No matter what country we look at, when citizens go to the polling stations, they always decide based on the same set of factors:

- their wallets, i.e., their economic self-interest;
- their conscience, religion, patriotism, tradition, family, and so on;
- their political beliefs or a particular party agenda.

Seventh, although the decision-making process in direct democracy is longer than in parliamentary democracy, the number of new laws created by the government would be significantly smaller. They would be filtered through the democratic instruments of civil control. Moreover, the Constitution would finally regain its power as the supreme law of the country and the source of citizens rights, as well as duties. The art of proper governance is to respect the Constitution and to make humane laws that are consulted with society. Essentially, it is about the quality and efficiency, not quantity and haste.

Eighth, the instruments of grassroots democracy make corruption limited or impossible. They prevent economic scandals, politicians' unlawful financial gains and wastefulness, stealing away of national assets, and dividing society into superior or inferior groups.

Afterword

Is the implementation of the instruments of direct democracy a utopian idea, or is it a chance for a better future of millions of Poles? And in others countries?

Frankly speaking, we do not have much to lose, rather we could build a truly democratic political system, in which citizens are no longer pawns on a chessboard used by incompetent and ill-willed players. The instruments of grassroots democracy (referendum, popular initiative and veto) would ensure a more efficient decision-making process and allow society to properly control politicians' actions.

If we managed to do this, everyone would find it easier to say things like: "It is my country," "It is my decision," "It is my motherland." Such words would have a true meaning and would not carry any false grandiloquence.

With time, these foundations would give rise to a genuine civil society, one that is socialised, pragmatic, engaged and actually participates in the political process. Without it a true democracy has no chance of survival, and *vice versa* – there will be no civil society without real grassroots democracy.

The model of democratic change in Poland presented in this book requires an amendment of the Constitution. However, this change – as a political project – has to be initiated outside the sphere of politics. It has to come from the people, and in order for that to happen, there has to occur a change in the mentality of Polish society. We cannot delude ourselves that the political elites will ever agree to such reforms of their own will. They see the people as "a mob," who cannot be let near the reins of power. Therefore, citizens are the ones who should realise that they are the sovereign, and that they should fight for their right to participate in the governance of the country.

The current Constitution is very convenient for the ruling elites. It is ambiguous, imprecise, inconsistent, and hedged around with so many laws that it can be interpreted in any way. This is especially visible in politicians' tendency to introduce many electoral thresholds. If there is a proposition of a reform that they consider as potentially harmful to their interests, they simply make it more difficult to reach the validity threshold – by hindering the debate and discouraging people from supporting the project – instead of honestly winning anyone over by persuasion.

Another interesting element of the Constitution is Article 7 that determines the principles governing the functioning of the state agencies. According to it, "The organs of public authority shall function on

the basis of, and within the limits of, the law." Our political elites use it to push the idea that the law is always right, which, in effect, undermines our legal system as a whole… This means that politicians can make any laws they want and justify them by simply pointing to Article 7.

It is a vicious circle. The only way to break it is to remind Poles that they are the true sovereign and that participation in the political process is their natural, democratic right.

We must free the Polish culture from the false notion that political power is something that can be *given to*, *divided between* or *taken back* by an exclusive group of people. No one in a democratic country – apart from the sovereign, i.e., the civil society – has the privilege to take the absolute power. It is essential to convince citizens that things can be different and better.

We do not need a revolution. What we need is an evolution that would spread the awareness of the fact that Poland belongs to us. We will not transform our semi-democracy by simply electing different people and political parties. The system has been flawed from the moment it was established 30 years ago. The question is: how long can it last?

It is not about looking for "good" politicians and condemning the "bad" ones. What we essentially need to do is to propose a simplified theoretical model of systemic choices and challenges necessary to improve the political system in Poland. Theory and practice show that we do not have to choose between "liberal parliamentarism" and "grassroots democracy. For it is impossible to state *a priori* that the latter or the former will turn out to be completely functional or dysfunctional. Political systems comprise of numerous elements, and one of the most important is a factor that I call "both this and that" which is essentially the fact that in order to come up with a healthy political process a country needs social dialogue and compromise above all. And this should be the foundation of the political process of the Polish state. Our model of a system based on grassroots democracy in no way suggests that we should copy the Swiss system in its entirety and implement it in Poland. It only points out that it is possible to combine elements of parliamentary and direct democracy. The result would be a complementary system, in which citizens would have a greater control over their country.

Does this book make the idea of grassroots democracy in Poland and in others countries more realistic? Is it a utopia or a chance? Is it only a charity for the people on the part of those in power, or is it a natural, democratic right of citizens?

I leave the answers to the Readers and Citizens.

Annexes

Annex I

Switzerland – Facts and Numbers

Name: Swiss Confederation (*Confoederatio Helvetica, Schweiz, Schweizerische Eidgenossenschaft*)
Capital: Berne
Largest cities: Zürich, Geneva, Basel, Berne
Neighbouring countries: Germany, France, Italy, Austria, Liechtenstein
Borders' length: 1,881 km
Area: 41,285 km²
Population: 8.2 million
Government: a federated state since 1848, parliamentary direct democracy
Administrative divisions: 20 cantons, 6 half-cantons: Aargau, Appenzell Ausserrhoden, Appenzell Innerrhoden, Basel-Landschaft, Basel-Stadt, Berne, Fribourg, Geneva, Jura, Luzern, Neuchâtel, Nidwalden, Obwalden, Schaffhausen, Schwyz, Solothurn, St. Gallen, Thurgau, Ticino, Uri, Valais, Vaud, Zug, Zürich
Currency: Swiss franc (= 100 centimes)

Languages: German (64 percent), French (19 percent), Italian (8 percent), Romansh (1 percent), others (8 percent)

Religion: Roman-Catholic (38 percent), Protestant (26 percent), Islam (5 percent), Irreligion (23 percent), others (8 percent)

Highest point: Dufourspitze in the Monte Rosa Massif: 4634 m

Lowest point: Lago Maggiore (Ticino): 193 m

Lakes: 1,484

Largest lakes: Lake Geneva, Lake Constance, Lake Neuchâtel, Lago Maggiore

Largest glaciers: Aletsch Glacier, Gorner Glacier, Fiescher Glacier, Aare Glaciers

Longest rivers: Rhine, Aare, Rhône, Reuss

National holiday: 1 August, the day when the cantons of Uri, Schwyz, and Unterwalden formed the alliance of 1291 on the Rütli mountain

The country's name comes from the canton of Schwyz – one of the founding cantons of the alliance of 1291. "CH" is an abbreviation for *Confoederatio Helvetica*.

Switzerland is a member of the United Nations (since 10 September 2002) and the European Free Trade Association. It is not a member of the European Union and the European Economic Area.

Annex II

The Federal Constitution of the Swiss Confederation (Titles I and IV)

Preamble

In the name of Almighty God!

The Swiss People and the Cantons, mindful of their responsibility towards creation, resolved to renew their alliance so as to strengthen liberty, democracy, independence and peace in a spirit of solidarity and openness towards the world, determined to live together with mutual consideration and respect for their diversity, conscious of their common achievements and their responsibility towards future generations and in the knowledge that only those who use their freedom remain free, and that the strength of a people is measured by the well-being of its weakest members, *adopt the following Constitution*:

Title 1: General Provisions

Art. 1. The Swiss Confederation

The People and the Cantons of Zurich, Bern, Lucerne, Uri, Schwyz, Obwalden and Nidwalden,

Glarus, Zug, Fribourg, Solothurn, Basel Stadt and Basel Landschaft, Schaffhausen, Appenzell Ausserrhoden and Appenzell Innerrhoden, St. Gallen, Graubünden, Aargau, Thurgau, Ticino, Vaud, Valais, Neuchâtel, Geneva, and Jura form the Swiss Confederation.

Art. 2. Aims
1. The Swiss Confederation shall protect the liberty and rights of the people and safeguard the independence and security of the country.
2. It shall promote the common welfare, sustainable development, internal cohesion and cultural diversity of the country.
3. It shall ensure the greatest possible equality of opportunity among its citizens.
4. It is committed to the long-term preservation of natural resources and to a just and peaceful international order.

Art. 3. Cantons
The Cantons are sovereign except to the extent that their sovereignty is limited by the Federal Constitution. They exercise all rights that are not vested in the Confederation.

Art. 4. National languages
The National Languages are German, French, Italian, and Romansh.

Art. 5. Rule of law

1. All activities of the state are based on and limited by law.
2. State activities must be conducted in the public interest and be proportionate to the ends sought.
3. State institutions and private persons shall act in good faith.
4. The Confederation and the Cantons shall respect international law.

Art. 5a. Subsidiarity

The principle of subsidiarity must be observed in the allocation and performance of state tasks.

Art. 6. Individual and collective responsibility

All individuals shall take responsibility for themselves and shall, according to their abilities, contribute to achieving the tasks of the state and society.

Title 4: The People and the Cantons

Chapter 1. General Provisions

Art. 136. Political rights

1. All Swiss citizens over the age of eighteen, unless they lack legal capacity due to mental illness or mental incapacity, have political rights in federal matters. All citizens have the same political rights and duties.

2. They may participate in elections to the National Council and in federal popular votes, and launch or sign popular initiatives and requests for referendums in federal matters.

Art. 137. Political parties
The political parties shall contribute to forming the opinion and will of the People.

Chapter 2. Initiative and Referendum

Art. 138. Popular initiative requesting the total revision of the Federal Constitution
1. Any 100,000 persons eligible to vote may within 18 months of the official publication of their initiative propose a total revision of the Federal Constitution.
2. This proposal must be submitted to a vote of the People.

Art. 139. Popular initiative requesting a partial revision of the Federal Constitution in specific terms
1. Any 100,000 persons eligible to vote may within 18 months of the official publication of their initiative request a partial revision of the Federal Constitution.
2. A popular initiative for the partial revision of the Federal Constitution may take the form of

a general proposal or of a specific draft of the provisions proposed.

3. If the initiative fails to comply with the requirements of consistency of form, and of subject matter, or if it infringes mandatory provisions of international law, the Federal Assembly shall declare it to be invalid in whole or in part.

4. If the Federal Assembly is in agreement with an initiative in the form of a general proposal, it shall draft the partial revision on the basis of the initiative and submit it to the vote of the People and the Cantons. If the Federal Assembly rejects the initiative, it shall submit it to a vote of the People; the People shall decide whether the initiative should be adopted. If they vote in favour, the Federal Assembly shall draft the corresponding bill.

5. An initiative in the form of a specific draft shall be submitted to the vote of the People and the Cantons. The Federal Assembly shall recommend whether the initiative should be adopted or rejected. It may submit a counter-proposal to the initiative.

Art. 139b. Procedure applicable to an initiative and counter-proposal

1. The People vote on the initiative and the counter-proposal at the same time.

2.   The People may vote in favour of both proposals. In response to the third question, they may indicate the proposal that they prefer if both are accepted.
3.   If in response to the third question one proposal to amend the Constitution receives more votes from the People and the other more votes from the Cantons, the proposal that comes into force is that which achieves the higher sum if the percentage of votes of the People and the percentage of votes of the Cantons in the third question are added together.

Art. 140. Mandatory referendum
1.   The following must be put to the vote of the People and the Cantons:
     a)   amendments to the Federal Constitution;
     b)   accession to organisations for collective security or to supranational communities;
     c)   emergency federal acts that are not based on a provision of the Constitution and whose term of validity exceeds one year; such federal acts must be put to the vote within one year of being passed by the Federal Assembly.
2.   The following are submitted to a vote of the People:
a)   popular initiatives for a total revision of the Federal Constitution;
b)   popular initiatives for a partial revision of the Federal Constitution in the form of a general proposal that have been rejected by the Federal Assembly;

c) the question of whether a total revision of the Federal Constitution should be carried out, in the event that there is disagreement between the two Councils.

Art. 141. Optional referendum

1. If within 100 days of the official publication of the enactment any 50,000 persons eligible to vote or any eight Cantons request it, the following shall be submitted to a vote of the People:
    a) federal acts;
    b) emergency federal acts whose term of validity exceeds one year;
    c) federal decrees, provided the Constitution or an act so requires;
    d) international treaties that:
1. are of unlimited duration and may not be terminated,
2. provide for accession to an international organisation,
3. contain important legislative provisions or whose implementation requires the enactment of federal legislation.

Art. 141a. Implementation of international treaties

1. If the decision on ratification of an international treaty is subject to a mandatory referendum, the Federal Assembly may incorporate in the decision on ratification the amendments to the

Constitution that provide for the implementation of the treaty.

2. If the decision on ratification of an international treaty is subject to an optional referendum, the Federal Assembly may incorporate in the decision on ratification the amendments to the law that provide for the implementation of the treaty.

Art. 142. Required majorities

1. Proposals that are submitted to the vote of the People are accepted if a majority of those who vote approve them.
2. Proposals that are submitted to the vote of the People and Cantons are accepted if a majority of those who vote and a majority of the Cantons approve them.
3. The result of a popular vote in a Canton determines the vote of the Canton.
4. The Cantons of Obwalden, Nidwalden, Basel-Stadt, Basel-Landschaft, Appenzell Ausserrhoden and Appenzell Innerrhoden each have half a cantonal vote.

Annex III

The Constitution of the Republic of Poland of 2nd April, 1997

(Articles: 4, 7, 90, 118, 125, 170, 221, 235)

Article 4 (forms of governance)
1. Supreme power in the Republic of Poland shall be vested in the Nation.
2. The Nation shall exercise such power directly or through their representatives.

Article 7 (the principle determining the mode of operation of state's agencies)
The organs of public authority shall function on the basis of, and within the limits of, the law.

Article 90 (delegation of competences to an international organisation)
1. The Republic of Poland may, by virtue of international agreements, delegate to an international organisation or international institution the competence of organs of State authority in relation to certain matters.

2. A statute, granting consent for ratification of an international agreement referred to in para. 1, shall be passed by the Sejm by a two-thirds majority vote in the presence of at least half of the statutory number of Deputies, and by the Senate by a two-thirds majority vote in the presence of at least half of the statutory number of Senators.

3. Granting of consent for ratification of such agreement may also be passed by a nationwide referendum in accordance with the provisions of Article 125.

4. Any resolution in respect of the choice of procedure for granting consent to ratification shall be taken by the Sejm by an absolute majority vote taken in the presence of at least half of the statutory number of Deputies.

Article 118 (legislative initiative)

1. The right to introduce legislation shall belong to Deputies, to the Senate, to the President of the Republic and to the Council of Ministers.

2. The right to introduce legislation shall also belong to a group of at least 100,000 citizens having the right to vote in elections to the Sejm. The procedure in such matter shall be specified by statute.

3. Sponsors, when introducing a bill to the Sejm, shall indicate the financial consequences of its implementation.

Article 125 (nationwide referendum)

1. A nationwide referendum may be held in respect of matters of particular importance to the State.
2. The right to order a nationwide referendum shall be vested in the Sejm, to be taken by an absolute majority of votes in the presence of at least half of the statutory number of Deputies, or in the President of the Republic with the consent of the Senate given by an absolute majority vote taken in the presence of at least half of the statutory number of Senators.
3. A result of a nationwide referendum shall be binding, if more than half of the number of those having the right to vote have participated in it.
4. The validity of a nationwide referendum and the referendum referred to in Article 235, para. 6., shall be determined by the Supreme Court.
5. The principles of and procedures for the holding of a referendum shall be specified by statute.

Article 170 (local referendum)

Members of a self-governing community may decide, by means of a referendum, matters concerning their community, including the dismissal of an organ of local government established by direct election. The principles of and procedures for conducting a local referendum shall be specified by statute.

Article 221 (legislative initiative regarding a Budget)
The right to introduce legislation concerning a Budget, a interim budget, amendments to the Budget, a statute on the contracting of public debt, as well as a statute granting financial guarantees by the State, shall belong exclusively to the Council of Ministers.

Article 235 (amending the Constitution)
1. A bill to ament the Constitution may be submitted by the following: at least one-fifth of the statutory number of Deputies; the Senate; or the President of the Republic.
2. Amendments to the Constitution shall be made by means of a statute adopted by the Sejm and, thereafter, adopted in the same wording by the Senate within a period of 60 days.
3. The first reading of a bill to amend the Constitution may take place no sooner than 30 days after the submission of the bill to the Sejm.
4. A bill to amend the Constitution shall be adopted by the Sejm by a majority of at least two-thirds of votes in the presence of at least half of the statutory number of Deputies, and by the Senate by an absolute majority of votes in the presence of at least half of the statutory number of Senators.
5. The adoption by the Sejm of a bill amending the provisions of Chapters I, II or XII of the

Constitution shall take place no sooner than 60 days after the first reading of the bill.

6. If a bill to amend the Constitution relates to the provisions of Chapters I, II or XII, the subjects specified in para. 1 above may require, within 45 days of the adoption of the bill by the Senate, the holding of a confirmatory referendum. Such subjects shall make application in the matter to the Marshal of the Sejm, who shall order the holding of a referendum within 60 days of the day or receipt of the application. The amendment to the Constitution shall be deemed accepted if the majority of those voting express support for such amendment.

7. After conclusion of the procedures specified in paras 4 and 6 above, the Marshal of the Sejm shall submit the adopted to the President of the Republic for signature. The President of the Republic shall sign the statute within 21 days of its submission and order its promulgation in the Journal of Laws of the Republic of Poland (*Dziennik Ustaw*).

Annex IV

Swiss Political System – Overview[44]

Political Levels

- Three political levels share power in Switzerland: the Confederation, the 26 cantons and over 2,250 communes.
- The Swiss federal government, (the Federal Council), is made up of seven members, who are elected by parliament.
- The Swiss parliament, or (Federal Assembly), has a total of 246 members, who are directly elected by the people. Switzerland has a bicameral parliament: the National Council (200 members) and the Council of States (46 members).
- 15 political parties are represented in the Swiss parliament. Those parties with the largest share of the popular vote are represented on the Federal Council.

---

[44] See: https://www.eda.admin.ch/aboutswitzerland/en/home/politik/ uebersicht/bundesrat.html (accesed 27.11.2018).

- Some 5.3 million citizens, roughly 63% of the total population, are eligible to vote at federal level. This right is granted to all Swiss nationals on reaching the age of majority (18 in Switzerland).

Political Parties

Some political parties are only active at a regional level, while others are well-rooted nationwide and have elected representatives in the Federal Assembly (parliament). The largest parties are represented in the Federal Council (cabinet).

Four parties dominate the Swiss political landscape. They are active in almost all 26 cantons and each have at least one representative in the Federal Council. According to the consociational model of democracy adopted in Switzerland, left-wing, right-wing and centrist parties all share executive power. Members of the Federal Council are drawn from the ranks of the Swiss People's Party (SVP), the Swiss Social Democratic Party (SP), the Christian Democrat People's Party (CVP) and the Liberals (FDP).

Although the Swiss Green Party (the Greens), the Swiss Green Liberal Party (the Green Liberals), the Conservative Democratic Party (BDP), the Lega dei Ticinesi, the Swiss Evangelical People's Party (EVP), the Christian Social Party (CSP) and the Geneva Citizens' Movement (MCG) may not be represented on the Federal Council, they have elected representatives in the federal parliament. The Conservative Democratic Party (BDP) was set up by former members of the SVP.

Over the last 20 years Switzerland's political landscape has been marked by the considerable gains made by the SVP, a conservative party which has its roots in the farming community. These gains have been at the expense of Switzerland's other right-wing parties. Between the federal elections of 1995 and those held in 2015, the SVP won an additional 36 parliamentary seats, while the FDP lost 12 and the CVP 10.

At the same time, considerable inroads have been made by the Greens (1995: 8 seats, 2015: 12 seats) and the Green Liberals (1995: 0 seats, 2015: 7 seats). The BDP, which was founded in 2008 by former SVP members, now has 8 members of parliament and has won a large number of cantonal and communal parliamentary seats.

In Switzerland, the primary source of funding for political parties is membership fees and donations. There is no federal obligation for parties to disclose their accounts or their donors. However, the cantons of Geneva, Neuchâtel and Ticino have each introduced their own party funding rules.

Federalism

Switzerland is made up of 26 cantons, which are themselves divided into more than 2,300 communes.

The Confederation, the cantons and communes share political and legislative powers.

Parliamentary chamber: the National Council © FDFA, Presence Switzerland

Although its official name is the Swiss Confederation (for historical reasons), Switzerland has, in fact, been a federal state since 1848. Power is shared between the Confederation (the central state based in the capital city of Bern), the cantons (constituent states) and the communes. All three political levels have a legislative (law-making) and an executive (government). Only the Confederation and the cantons have judicial powers (courts).

In a country with different religious and linguistic groups, the federalism model makes it possible to accommodate both national unity and cultural diversity. Together with direct democracy, which offers the people the option of launching popular initiatives and referendums, federalism is one of the cornerstones of the Swiss political system.

To ensure that the 26 cantons are equally represented at the federal level, each canton sends two representatives to the Council of States, one of the two chambers of the Federal Assembly. The six half-cantons are an exception to this rule, and can send only one elected representative to Bern. All 26 cantons have the right to launch a popular referendum on a piece of federal legislation provided that at least eight cantons express support for it.

The powers of the Confederation are limited to those areas explicitly entrusted to it by the Federal Constitution. Responsibility for all other matters, such as education, health and policing, fall to the cantons, which enjoy a high degree of policy-making autonomy in these areas. As for the communes, their responsibilities are explicitly granted by either the canton or the Confederation. However, the communes may legislate on matters that are not covered by cantonal legislation.

The Federal Council

The Federal Council is the highest executive authority of the Swiss Confederation. Its members represent Switzerland's main political parties.

The Swiss Federal Council 2018 (left to right): Federal Councillor Guy Parmelin, Federal Councillor Simonetta Sommaruga, Federal Councillor Ueli Maurer (vice-president of the Federal Council), President of the Confederation Alain Berset, Federal Councillor Doris Leuthard, Federal Councillor Johann N. Schneider-Ammann, Federal Councillor Ignazio Cassis, Federal Chancellor Walter Thurnherr.

The national government of Switzerland has seven members, who are elected by the United Federal Assembly. Each Federal Councillor is appointed to serve a one-year term as President of the Confederation by the Federal Assembly in accordance with the principle of seniority. The Federal President chairs the sessions of the executive and undertakes special ceremonial duties, particularly abroad.

In keeping with the consociational model of democracy adopted by Switzerland, all members of the Federal Council pledge to govern in a spirit of cooperation. As a collegial body, the Federal Council must remain unanimous when presenting cabinet decisions to the public, even if it is contrary to their personal view or to the official line taken by their party.

Composition and roles

At the present time, the Federal Council has two representatives from the Liberal Party (FDP), two representatives from the Swiss Social Democratic Party (SP), two representatives from the Swiss People's Party (SVP), and one representative from the Swiss Christian Democratic Party (CVP). Each member of the Federal Council also heads a federal department.

The Federal Council generally meets once a week. Over the year, it deals with between 2,000 and 2,500 items of business, which have been prepared by the federal departments or by the Federal Chancellery. The Federal Chancellor, who acts as chief-of-staff to the Federal Council, attends all cabinet meetings, but in a purely advisory capacity.

The Federal Assembly (parliament)

Switzerland has a bicameral parliament. All 246 members are directly elected by the people.

The Federal Assembly is the legislative power of Switzerland. Its two chambers – the National Council and the Council of States –have the same powers but meet separately.

The National Council, or "lower chamber", represents the people and comprises 200 members who are elected by popular vote for a four-year term. The number of representatives sent by each canton depends on the size of its population. As a rule of thumb, each canton may send one elected representative to the National Council for roughly every 40,000 inhabitants.

The Federal Constitution guarantees at least one seat per canton, even if the canton has fewer than 40,000 residents. The cantons of Appenzell-Ausserrhoden, Appenzell-Innerrhoden, Obwalden, Nidwalden, Uri and Glarus send one National Council member each, whereas Zurich, the most heavily populated canton, currently has 35 seats.

The Council of States, or "upper chamber", represents the cantons and comprises 46 members, who are also elected directly by the people for a four-year term. Regardless of their population size, the cantons send two deputies, with the exception of the six half-cantons of Appenzell-Ausserrhoden, Appenzell-Innerrhoden, Obwalden,

Nidwalden, Basel-Stadt and Basel-Land, which send one deputy each.

Council of States deputies represent their cantons but are not bound by any instructions from their cantonal government or parliament.

Role and powers of the Swiss parliament
The National Council and the Council of States meet for three-week sessions four times a year. The two chambers debate all constitutional amendments before putting them to the popular vote. They also adopt, amend or repeal federal legislation, and ratify international treaties.

The two parliamentary chambers sit together as the United Federal Assembly at least once a year, usually in December, in order to elect the members of the Federal Council and to appoint federal court judges.

The Federal Assembly is, in keeping with the Swiss "militia" concept of community service, a semi-professional parliament. This means that most deputies have another job in addition to their parliamentary duties, to which they devote an average of 60% of their working hours.

Direct Democracy

Direct democracy is one of the special features of the Swiss political system. It allows the electorate to express their opinion on decisions taken by the federal parliament and to propose amendments to the Federal Constitution.

Completing a ballot paper © FDFA, Presence Switzerland

In Switzerland the people play a large part in the federal political decision-making process. All Swiss citizens aged 18 and over have the right to vote in elections and referendums. The Swiss electorate are called on approximately four times a year to exercise this right, and vote on an average of 15 federal proposals. In recent decades, voter turnout at elections and referendums has been below 40%.

As well as the right to vote in elections and referendums, Swiss citizens may voice their demands by means of three instruments which form the core of direct democracy: popular initiative, optional referendum and mandatory referendum.

Popular initiative

The popular initiative gives citizens the right to propose an amendment or addition to the Constitution. It acts to drive or launch a political debate on a specific issue. For such an initiative to come about, the signatures of 100,000 voters who support the proposal must be collected within 18 months. The authorities sometimes respond to an initiative with a direct counter-proposal in the hope that a majority of the people and the cantons support that instead.

Optional referendum

The optional referendum allows the people to demand that any bill approved by the Federal Assembly is put to a nationwide vote. In order to bring about a national referendum, 50,000 valid signatures must be collected within 100 days of publication of the new legislation.

Mandatory referendum

All constitutional amendments approved by parliament are subject to a mandatory referendum, i.e. they must be put to a nationwide popular vote. The electorate are also required to approve Swiss membership of specific international organisations.

The Cantons

Switzerland is made up of 26 cantons which enjoy a high degree of autonomy vis-à-vis the federal government.

The dome of the Federal Palace © The Swiss Parliament

Switzerland is divided into 26 cantons. Each is an independent and sovereign entity, with their own capital town or city. The cantons vary greatly as to size, culture, religion and socioeconomic structure.

With 1.4 million inhabitants, the canton of Zurich is the most heavily populated, while Appenzell-Innerrhoden, with a mere 15,500 inhabitants, is the most sparsely populated canton in Switzerland.

Origins

The cantons are the collection of stand-alone states which joined forces in 1848 to form a Confederation, although this required them to surrender some of their sovereignty. The number of cantons remained the same until 1979 when Jura split from the canton of Bern and became Switzerland's 26th canton.

Six cantons, historically referred to as "half-cantons", send only one deputy to the Council of States (upper house of the Federal Assembly). They are Obwalden, Nidwalden, Appenzell-Innerrhoden, Appenzell-Ausserrhoden, Basel-Stadt and Basel-Land.

Role of the cantons

Each canton has its own constitution, parliament, government and courts. According to the principle of subsidiarity enshrined in the Federal Constitution, all powers that are not expressly granted to the Confederation fall within the competence of the cantons. The cantons enjoy a high degree of autonomy in areas like education, health and policing.

The cantonal parliaments vary in size, with the number of popularly elected deputies ranging from 50 to 180. The five- or seven-member cantonal governments are also directly elected by the people.

The cantons of Appenzell-Innerrhoden and Glarus still practice a type of direct democracy that is the only form of its kind in the world – the

"Landsgemeinde", or people's assembly. Once a year, the citizens of these cantons converge on their capital›s main square to elect, with a show of hands, the members of the executive, and to cast their vote on draft cantonal legislation. The results are more an estimate than an exact calculation. In all other cantons, the electorate cast their vote at the ballot box.

Annex V

Frequently Asked Questions

1. **Will the ruling class agree to "give power back to society"?**

It does not have to "agree" since power already belongs to the People. The ruling class that controls the fate of nearly 40 million Poles must simply accept the introduction of certain elements of grassroots democracy into current form of governing. Such a change would definitely not overturn the political system but it would complement and upgrade it so that the state would become more humane and democratic. It is impossible to give, take away, or appropriate power in a truly democratic system.

2. **Is Polish society "mature" enough for this kind of democracy?**

After centuries of experiencing different political systems, Polish society does not have to prove anything to be worthy of democracy. If a nation is prevented from participating in power, it will never develop into civil society, and – *vice versa* – a true democracy will not function properly without citizens' active participation. Apart from that, Poles certainly do not need lessons in patriotism or Christian ethics.

3. Does not grassroots democracy, as a political process, take too much time to accomplish anything?

The decision-making process in a direct democracy is longer than in a parliamentary one. Judging by the example of Switzerland, however, it results in a smaller number of hasty decisions. Such a system has certain advantages: decisions are made in a thoughtful manner and filtered by society as a whole, instead of being pushed by a limited circle of politicians. Decisions made by citizens at the polling stations have a wider social support and acceptance, which makes them more democratic and effective.

4. Would not a grassroots democracy be too expensive for Poland?

When asking about costs, we usually mean administrative expenditures in a given system. Therefore, the proper question is: what would be the cost of organising an initiative, a veto, or a referendum? If we consider the socio-economic costs of bad decisions made under the current system, a grassroots democracy presents itself as incomparably cheaper. Let us remind ourselves how much of our national assets were sold off in the early '90s. If there had been a referendum on this during that time, Poland would not be in the hands of foreign corporations today.

5. Will "giving back power to the People" lead to irresponsible management of national assets?

It is a simplistic way of thinking. It would seem that grassroots democracy gives citizens the possibility to initiate the most unrealistic projects and to veto any opposing voices. However, the very act of collecting signatures makes the process rather difficult. Moreover, decisions are made by society as a whole in a referendum preceded by an informative campaign in which all interested parties present their viewpoint. It should be also remembered that it is also society itself that will bare any consequences. Finally, maybe it would be more proper to ask ironically: is the Nation capable of wasting national assets more than it has been done by our politicians for the last 30 years?

6. How to harmonise the supremacy of EU laws over national laws in a grassroots democracy?

Being a member state means that EU's laws are superior to the national law of Poland. Therefore, any projects of amending the Constitution (or a statute) have to be in accordance with the Union's law. The government should verify the legal compatibility of an initiative or a veto before any signatures are collected. This applies not only to the laws of the EU but also to any international laws that Poland has obliged to follow.

7. **Is not it to soon to introduce any elements of direct democracy in Poland?**

Certainly not. Let us take a look a the Polish semi-democracy of the last 30 years. Where are we now? The elements of grassroots democracy are a chance to heal Poland's socio-political and economic system. The sooner, the better for everyone.

8. **Would introduction of grassroots democracy undermine the role of state's institutions and political parties?**

It would hardly be the case. They would become more democratic and be compelled to consider the will of society. It is certain, however, that the authoritarian mode of governing by the current elites would be eliminated – it is their position, not the state's institutions as such, that would be undermined. Political parties would have to re-evaluate their role since they would not be the sole middleman between the state's institutions and society anymore. Moreover, they would no longer be considered as the only agencies capable of improving the socio-economic situation of the country.

9. **Does a referendum without a validity threshold truly reflect the views of the majority (or all) citizens?**

The idea of a referendum with a validity threshold is an unjustified and undemocratic invention of the Polish ruling class. If a person does not participate in a referendum, it should be considered as an equally valid, although passive, voice. Apart from that, different referenda will attract different social groups – while some people will find a particular problem urgent, others will see it as unimportant. Thus, when it comes to a referendum the voter turnout should be irrelevant. Let us remember that even if only a minority of citizens participates in voting, they still constitute a larger group – in terms of single individuals – than the number of representatives in the Sejm. A true democracy will always stand on its own merits and be able to seize the future.

10. Can a single citizen initiate the legislative process?

Yes, by all means. A individual can, for example, establish an initiating committee and promote a particular project. Of course, in order to make it effective, it is necessary to collect the required number of signatures. The final decision will nevertheless be made by all citizens eligible to vote.

11. Why is it that the discussion about the possibility of grassroots democracy in Poland has started only now?

There are several reasons. **First,** the contemporary Poland lacks the tradition of grassroots form of governance. Polish society has been ruled in an authoritarian and egoistic manner for decades. Any changes were simply cosmetic. Thus, it is difficult for Polish citizens to imagine a situation in which they are not governed by others. **Second,** grassroots democracy limits the possibilities of gaining power by shady elites and celebrities. In such system politicians' pompous slogans of patriotism, tradition, and ideology, which serve as a cover-up for corruption, lose their power. Instead, organic work carried out by carious groups becomes the foundation of the people's awareness of their true interests. Moreover, grassroots democracy significantly alters the nature of political power, i.e., the process in which certain individuals dominate over masses. That is why politicians do not want to share whatever power they have with average citizens. **Third,** the young Polish democracy has assumed its current parliamentary-elitist form already after the country's systemic transformation. It is understandable since thirty years ago everybody was eager to accept any form of democracy that would replace the socialist "people's democracy." The experience of the last three decades, however, has shown that the current semi-democracy does not meet the expectations of Polish society. **Fourth,** the simplicity of a complementary democracy that enables citizens to participate in the process of governance is, paradoxically, beyond the comprehension of the currently ruling class.

Annex VI

Basic Terms

Referendum – a form of general voting that is the closest embodiment of direct democracy in which all citizens eligible to vote (active suffrage) can participate. During a referendum citizens of a country (or its part) articulate their opinion on a certain issue. As an instrument, it allows to control the government's actions, shape the political system and express the will of society.

Popular veto – a political instrument that allows citizens to express their objections regarding the solutions existing in a country's legal system. In practice it means that a certain number of citizens eligible to vote may, within a given period, make an official stance concerning a particular statute. Following this, society votes on the matter ("yes" or "no") in a referendum. Popular veto has a direct impact on the political process by enabling a grassroots, civil control over the decisions made by the state's authorities.

Popular initiative – a political instrument that grants citizens and socio-political groups the right to propose laws. Its practical implementations differ among various countries. In Switzerland, it may concern a partial or complete amendment of the constitution, provided that the project is supported by a required number of citizens eligible to vote who, within a specific period, collect necessary signatures. They can demand to introduce simple amendments or repeal existing provisions, or propose a completely new solution. Popular initiative may concern both particular and general matters. It should be mentioned that any initiative with the required number of signatures has to be followed by a referendum.

Annex VII

A Simplified Model of Direct Democracy in Poland (© M. Matyja, Public Domain)

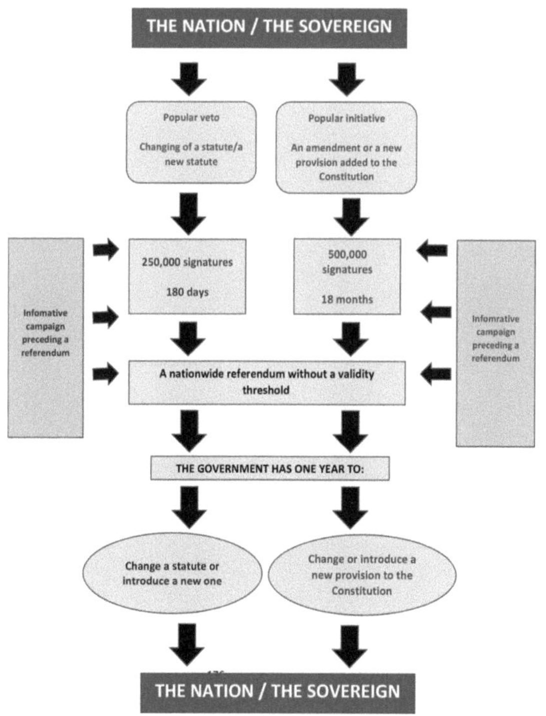

Selected bibliography

Monographs and articles:

1. Aleksandrowicz M., System prawny Szwajcarii: historia i współczesność, Białystok 2009.
2. Altermatt U., Konkordanz im Spiegel der Bundesratswahlen, [in:] A. Vatter, F. Varone, F. Sager (Hrsg.), Demokratie als Leidenschaft. Planung, Entscheidung und Vollzug in der schweizerischen Demokratie. Festschrift für Prof. Dr. Wolf Linder zum 65. Geburtstag, Haupt, Bern-Stuttgart-Wien 2009, p. 247–267.
3. Armingeon K., Direkte Demokratie als Exportartikel, [in:] Vatter, Adrian; Varone, Frédéric; Sager, Fritz (eds.) Demokratie als Leidenschaft. Planung, Entscheidung und Vollzug in der schweizerischen Demokratie. Festschrift für Prof. Dr. Wolf Linder zum 65. Geburtstag, Haupt, Bern 2009, p. 433–442.
4. Banaszak B., Porównawcze prawo konstytucyjne współczesnych państw demokratycznych, Warszawa 2007.

5. Bankowicz M., Demokracja. Zasady, procedury, instytucje, Kraków 2006.

6. Blöchliger H., Kantone – Baustelle Föderalismus. Metropolitanregionen versus Kantone. Untersuchungen und Vorschläge für eine Revitalisierung der Schweiz, NZZ Libro, Zürich 2005.

7. Braun N., Direct Democracy in Switzerland. Case Study, [in:] Direct Democracy. The International IDEA Handbook , Stockholm 2008.

8. Büchi Ch., Röstigraben. Das Verhältnis zwischen deutscher und welscher Schweiz. Geschichte und Perspektiven, NZZ, Zürich 2000.

9. Büchi R., Braun N., Kaufmann B., Przewodnik po demokracji bezpośredniej, Initiative & Referendum Institute Europe, Łódź 2013.

10. Czeszejko-Sochacki Z., System konstytucyjny Szwajcarii, Wydawnictwo Sejmowe, Warszawa 2002.

11. Czeszejko-Sochacki Z., Foreword, in: Konstytucja Federalna Konfederacji Szwajcarskiej z dnia 18 kwietnia 1999 r., transl. and foreword: Z. Czeszejko-Sochacki, Warszawa 2000.

12. Degen B., Referendum, [entry in:] Historisches Lexikon der Schweiz, Bd. 10: Pro-Schafroth, Schwabe, Basel 2011, p. 166–168.

13. Deszczyński P., Gołata K., Demokratyczne systemy polityczne, [in:] System parlamentarno-kantonalny Szwajcarii, ed. P. Deszczyński, Poznań 2000.

14. Eichenberger R., Starke Föderalismus. Drei Reformvorschläge für fruchtbaren Föderalismus, Orell Füssli, Zürich 2002.

15. Eine Schweiz – viele Religionen. Risiken und Chancen des Zusammenlebens, Hrsg. M. Baumann, J. Stolz, Transkript, Bielefeld 2007.

16. Élites politiques et peuple en Suisse. Analyse des votations fédérales. 1970–1987, ed. Y. Papadopoulos, Lausanne 1994.

17. Fenner M., Hadorn R., Strahm R. H., Politszene Schweiz. Politik und Wirtschaft heute , Verlag für Sozialwissenschaft, Basel 2000.

18. Frey R. L. (Hrsg.), Föderalismus – Zukunftstauglich?!, NZZ Libro, Zürich 2005.

19. Gabriel J. M., Das politische System der Schweiz, Haupt, Bern 1997.

20. Górski B., Jak przeżyć kapitalizm, Retro-Art, Warszawa 2013.

21. Grabowska S., Formy demokracji bezpośredniej w wybranych państwach europejskich, Rzeszów 2009.

22. Grenzen des Zumutbaren. Erfahrungen mit der französischen Okkupation und der Helvetischen Republik (1798–1803), Hrsg. A. Würgler, Schwabe Verl., Basel 2011.

23. Grodziski S., Porównawcza historia ustrojów państwowych, UNIVERSITAS, Kraków 1998.

24. Helg F., Die schweizerischen Landsgemeinden. Ihre staatsrechtliche Ausgestaltung in den Kantonen Appennzell Ausserrhoden, Appenzell Innerrhoden, Glarus, Nidwalden und Obwalden, Schulthess Juristische Medien AG, Zürich-Basel-Genf 2007.

25. Hug S., Occurrence and Policy Consequences of Referendums, "Journal of Theoretical Politics" 2004, vol. 16, p. 321–336.

26. Jakubowski W., Załęski P., Systemy polityczne państw Europy Zachodniej nie należących do Unii Europejskiej i wybranych państw pozaeuropejskich – Konfederacja Szwajcarska, [in:] Społeczeństwo i polityka. Podstawy nauk politycznych, K.A. Wojtaszczyk, W. Jakubowski (ed.), Warszawa 2003.

27. Kirchgässner G. et al., Die direkte Demokratie. Modern, erfolgreich, entwicklungs- und exportfähig, Helbing & Lichtenhahn, Vahlen, Basel-Genf-München 1999.

28. Kost A., Direkte Demokratie, Verlag für Sozialwissenschaft, Wiesbaden 2008.

29. Kriesi H., Le système politique suisse, Economica, Paris 1995.

30. Kutter M., Doch dann regiert das Volk. Ein Schweizer Beitrag zur Theorie der direkten Demokratie., Ammann Verlag, Zürich 1996.

31. Leupold M., Besson M., Gefährden Volksinitiativen die «gute Ordnung» der Verfassung?, LEGES 2011/3, p. 389 – 407.

32. Linder W., Demokracja szwajcarska, Rzeszów 1996.

33. Manatschal A., Kantonale Integrationspolitik im Vergleich. Eine Untersuchung der Determinanten und Auswirkungen subnationaler Politikvielfalt, Nomos, Baden-Baden 2013.

34. Marczewska-Rytko M., Szwajcarski model demokracji bezpośredniej, [in:] Stan i perspektywy demokracji bezpośredniej we współczesnym świecie, M. Marczewska-Rytko (ed.), Lublin 2011.

35. Marczewska-Rytko M., Inicjatywa ludowa i referendum w Szwajcarii w latach 2000--2010, „Polityka i Społeczeństwo" 2012, no. 9, p. 272–283.

36. Matsusaka J.G, The eclipse of legislatures. Direct democracy in the 21st c., „Public Choice" 2000, vol. 124, p. 157–177.

37. Matyja M, Federalism and multiethnicity in Switzerland, [in:] Essays on Regionalisation. Collection of reports submitted at the International Conference. Regionalisation in Southeast Europe. Comparative Analysis and Perspectives, ed. Agencija Lokalne Demokratije, Center – Agency of Local Democracy, Subotica 2001, p. 129–136.

38. Matyja M., Swiss Made. Jak funkcjonuje międzykulturowa Szwajcaria?, Poligraf, Brzezia Łąka 2010.

39. Matyja M., *Besonderheiten des politischen Systems der Schweiz. Föderalismus und direkte Demokratie*, „Europa Regionum" 2009, Bd. 12, p. 13–23.
40. Matyja M., *Szwajcarski system federalny*, „Stosunki Międzynarodowe", http://www.stosunki.pl/?q=content/szwajcarski-system-federalny [accessed 28.08.2017].
41. Matyja M., *Dysfunkcjonalność szwajcarskiej demokracji bezpośredniej*, Adam Marszalek, Torun 2016.
42. Matyja M., *Szwajcarska demokracja szansa dla Polski*, PAFERE, Warszawa 2018.
43. Matyja M., *Polska semidemokracja. Dylematy oddolnej demokracji w III Rzeczpospolitej*, WGP, Warszawa 2019.
44. Meyer T., *Was ist Demokratie*, Verlag für Sozialwissenschaft, Wiesbaden 2009.
45. Möckli S., *Funktionen und Dysfunktionen der direkten Demokratie*, „Beiträge und Berichte" 1995, No. 237.
46. Moeckli S., *Das politische System der Schweiz verstehen*, Tobler, Altstätten 2007.
47. Myślak E., *System polityczny Konfederacji Szwajcarskiej*, Wyd. UJ, Kraków 2014.
48. Musiał-Karg M., *Elektroniczne referendum w Szwajcarii. Wybrane kierunki zmian helweckiej demokracji bezpośredniej*, Wyd. WNPiD UAM, Poznań 2012.

49. Najstarsze konstytucje z końca XVIII i I połowy XIX wieku, transl. and foreword: P. Sarnecki, Warszawa 1997.

50. Neidhart L., Die politische Schweiz. Fundamente und Institutionen, NZZ Libro, Zürich 2002.

51. Podolak M., System polityczny Szwajcarii, [in:] Współczesne systemy polityczne, Żmigrodzki M, Dziemidok-Olszewska B. (ed.), PWN, Warszawa 2013.

52. Pogorzelska-Kliks Agata, Ewolucja tożsamości narodowej mieszkańców szwajcarskiego kantonu Valais, doctoral dissertation, Uniwersytet Śląski Wydział Nauk Społecznych, Katowice 2007.

53. Quermonne J.-L., Les régimes politiques occidentaux (The Western Political Systems), Editions du Seuil, Paryż 1994.

54. Roca R., Wenn die Volkssouveränität wirklich eine Wahrheit werden soll… Die schweizerische direkte Demokratie in Theorie und Praxis – Das Beispiel des Kantons Luzern, Schulthess Juristische Medien AG, Zürich/Basel/Genf 2012.

55. Rybicki M., Konstytucja Związkowa Konfederacji Szwajcarskiej, [in:] Konstytucje Wielkiej Brytanii, Stanów Zjednoczonych, Belgii i Szwajcarii, Wrocław 1970.

56. Sarnecki P., Zgromadzenie Federalne. Parlament Konfederacji Szwajcarskiej, Warszawa 2003.

57. Schulze H., *Państwo i naród w dziejach Europy*, przeł. D. Lachowska, Wyd. Uniwersytetu Warszawskiego, Warszawa 2012.
58. Sokół W., *System partyjny współczesnej Szwajcarii*, [in:] Annales UMCS, vol. V, 1998, p. 45–56.
59. Vatter A., *Das politische System der Schweiz*, Nomos, Baden-Baden 2014.
60. Vatter A., *Direkte Demokratie in der Schweiz. Entwicklungen, Debatten und Wirkungen*, [in:] *Direkte Demokratie. Bestandsaufnahmen und Wirkungen im internationalen Vergleich*, Hrsg. U. Wagschal, M. Freitag, LIT, Münster 2007.
61. Wójtowicz J., *Historia Szwajcarii*, Wrocław–Warszawa–Kraków–Gdańsk–Łódź 1989.
62. Zieliński E. (ed.), *Referendum w państwach Europy*, ASPRA 2005.

Encyclopaedias, dictionaries, lexicons:

1. Encyklopedia PWN, https://encyklopedia.pwn.pl/haslo/subsydiarnosc;4836984.html, (accessed 10.08.2017).
2. Historisches Lexikon der Schweiz, http://www.hls-dhs-dss.ch/textes/d/D9808.php, (accessed 09.08.2018).

The Press:

1. Neue Zürcher Zeitung from 11.03.2015: http://www.nzz.ch/schweiz/nationalrat-setzt-ausschaffungsinitiative-mit-haertefallklausel-um-1.18499799, (accessed 12.02.2019).
2. Sadurski W., Referendum nie jest dobre na wszystko, „Rzeczpospolita" 1998, no. 81.

Internet sources:

1. Bundesblatt no. 34 von 26. Juli 1873, http://www.admin.ch/opc/de/federal-gazette/1873/index_34.html, (accessed 10.08.2018).
2. Center for Research on Direct Democracy, http://www.c2d.ch/inner.php?table=country_information&su-blinkname=country_information&country-geo=1&le-vel=1&menuname=menu&continent=Europe, (accessed 20.08.2018).
3. Die Bundesverfassung von 1874, Historisches Lexikon der Schweiz, http://www.hls-dhs-dss.ch/textes/d/D9811.php, (accessed 10.08.2018).
4. Federal Statistical Office in Neuchâtel, http://www.bfs.admin.ch/bfs/portal/de/index/themen/17/03/blank/key/eidg__volksinitiativen.html, (accessed 10.09.2018).

5. Federal Statistical Office in Neuchâtel, http://www.bfs.admin.ch/bfs/portal/de/index/themen/17/03/blank/key/eidg__volksinitiativen.html, (accessed 21.08.2018).
6. Official website of Switzerland's federal government and administration: www.admin.ch, (accessed 21.08.2018).
7. Official website of Switzerland's federal parliament: www.parlament.ch, (accessed 21.08.2018).
8. Schweizerische Bundeskanzlei, Chronologie Abstimmungen, http://www.admin.ch/ch/d//pore/va/vab_2_2_4_1.html, (accessed 27.08.2018).
9. The Constitution of the Swiss Confederation: http://libr.sejm.gov.pl/tek01/txt/konst/szwajcaria.html (accessed 06.12.2018).

List of Figures

List of Tables